Praise for

If You Ask Me

"The America that emerges through this twenty-year sampling of Roosevelt's advice column is at once familiar and very long gone. We're still wrestling, of course, with arguments over civil liberties, national health care, the Electoral College, and institutionalized racism and sexism. Roosevelt gamely weighed in on those hot-button topics. But then there are a whole slew of other letters here that come out of an America so earnest it almost seems like the product of a work of speculative fiction. . . . There's something very democratic about this twenty-plus-year monthly 'conversation' of sorts."

—NPR's *Fresh Air*

"Heartwarming, smart, and at times even humorous, this book highlights a collection of Roosevelt's best columns and allows her warm wit and wisdom to shine as an uplifting and timely 'advice guide.'"

—*Woman's World*

"Roosevelt emerges as blunt and opinionated, but also open, compassionate, and genuinely interested in others. . . . Quotable and surprisingly timely, this optimistic book is both bracing and comforting."

—*Publishers Weekly*

If You Ask Me

Essential Advice from
Eleanor Roosevelt

ELEANOR ROOSEVELT

Based on the book *If You Ask Me* by Eleanor Roosevelt
with additional extracts from *Ladies Home Journal*
and *McCall's* columns drawn from the corpus edition
of The Eleanor Roosevelt Papers

Edited and with an Introduction by Mary Jo Binker

ATRIA PAPERBACK

NEW YORK • LONDON • TORONTO • SYDNEY • NEW DELHI

For Roland and Tony

ATRIA
PAPERBACK

An Imprint of Simon & Schuster, LLC
1230 Avenue of the Americas
New York, NY 10020

This Atria Paperback edition October 2024

ATRIA PAPERBACK and colophon are trademarks of Simon & Schuster, LLC

Simon & Schuster: Celebrating 100 Years of Publishing in 2024

For information about special discounts for bulk purchases, please contact Simon & Schuster Special Sales at 1-866-506-1949 or business@simonandschuster.com.

The Simon & Schuster Speakers Bureau can bring authors to your live event. For more information or to book an event contact the Simon & Schuster Speakers Bureau at 1-866-248-3049 or visit our website at www.simonspeakers.com.

Interior design by Dana Sloan

Manufactured in the United States of America

1 3 5 7 9 10 8 6 4 2

Library of Congress Cataloging-in-Publication Data

Names: Roosevelt, Eleanor, 1884-1962. | Binker, Mary Jo, editor.
Title: If you ask me : essential advice from Eleanor Roosevelt / edited and with an introduction by Mary Jo Binker.
Other titles: Ladies' home journal
Description: New York, NY : Atria Books, 2018. | "Adapted from a corpus edition of The Eleanor Roosevelt Papers"—Title page. | Includes bibliographical references and index. |
Identifiers: LCCN 2018029491 (print) | LCCN 2018033977 (ebook) | ISBN 9781501179815 (Ebook) | ISBN 9781501179792 (hardback)
Subjects: LCSH: Roosevelt, Eleanor, 1884-1962—Political and social views. | Advice columns. | Conduct of life. | BISAC: HISTORY / United States / 20th Century.
Classification: LCC E807.1.R48 (ebook) | LCC E807.1.R48 A42 2018 (print) | DDC 973.917092--dc23
LC record available at https://lccn.loc.gov/2018029491

ISBN 978-1-5011-7979-2
ISBN 978-1-5011-7980-8 (pbk)
ISBN 978-1-5011-7981-5 (ebook)

CONTENTS

FOREWORD

MY GRANDMOTHER ALWAYS encouraged keeping an open mind and seeking as many different opinions as one had time for. She claimed it helped to clarify her own thinking. Eleanor's story was a progression from timidity to self-confidence. She felt she could choose the right answer if given time for thoughtful deliberation and if she maintained respect for those around her even if she didn't share their views.

The passage of time has only proved how prescient she was. She saw clearly how things could change for the better, and she saw that the only possible solution was for people to take greater responsibility for their community, their country, and their world. Here, in *If You Ask Me,* she gives us advice both timeless and timely, worth reading for the time it grew out of as well as the timelessness of its observations on human nature and values.

Eleanor speaks to us from a familiar milieu: the Progressive Era and the Gilded Age—so gilded that wealthy white women, at least during daylight hours, left their townhouses en masse for the tenements of New York City's Lower East Side. It is easy to dismiss these privileged social reformers, but we should also remember their victories—child-labor and sanitation laws, women's suffrage, and contraceptive rights. Even Prohibition, though set against a backdrop of anti-immigrant zeal, was intended to combat a real culture of drug and alcohol abuse still destroying families today.

Eleanor was not a teetotaler. She drank socially, though not during Prohibition. She smoked because she sometimes felt it made others more comfortable for her to do so. She accepted the end of Prohibition as having been a foolhardy attempt to legislate morality, primarily because it had encouraged the consumption of spirits over wine and so made the problem only worse.

Grandmère knew that as First Lady people looked to her first as a symbol, but she infused a ceremonial role with warmth. As Franklin was president through the Great Depression and World War II, Eleanor provided a sign of continuity to rally around during uncertain times, representing the tenderhearted wing of her husband's administration. And yet, it is for the humanity of the New Deal and Franklin's accessibility in his fireside chats that the F.D.R. presidency is best remembered.

Because of her modesty, it is up to us to recognize that Eleanor Roosevelt fundamentally changed the role of First Lady. This transition is reflected in the book of questions and answers that follows. It's funny to read some of the early answers that appear wrongheaded now, and it's humbling to see how many are questions we are still grappling with today.

Throughout, Eleanor's wit and personality shine through. Her response to the mother of an adolescent girl who's grown tall too fast and feels gangly and awkward as a result is sweet to read when one knows how Eleanor struggled with the same feelings. People wrote to her as an authority on everything from foreign policy to raising adolescents, and she repaid this faith placed in her by treating every letter writer with respect and care.

The Reverend Martin Luther King, quoting a nineteenth-century theologian, said that "the arc of the moral universe is long, but it bends toward justice." Grandmère, an eternal optimist, would have agreed, chiefly because she had great faith in the ability and the willingness of people to ensure that it did so.

Nancy Roosevelt Ireland

INTRODUCTION

"**A**DVICE COLUMNIST" is not the first term that comes to mind when you think of Eleanor Roosevelt. Feminist icon, first lady, diplomat, humanitarian, politician, teacher—these are the more common ways she is described and remembered. Yet, for more than twenty years, from the time she was first lady until her death in 1962, she wrote an advice column that dealt with everything from how to achieve world peace to how to attain personal happiness. Her column, "If You Ask Me," was no empty public relations exercise designed to demonstrate her supposed empathy. She genuinely *cared* about people and their problems. Forthright, honest, and insightful, her answers to readers' queries are also surprisingly modern and strikingly relevant to our own tumultuous times.[1]

Although "If You Ask Me" launched her official career as an advice columnist, it was actually a natural extension of what Eleanor was already doing every day—spending hours answering her mail. Unlike most first ladies, Eleanor had actually *asked* Americans to write her. And they did, in droves. By 1940, near the end of her husband's second term, Eleanor estimated that she received upward of 130,000 letters a year.[2] Written during some of the worst years of the Great Depression, many of these early letters asked for practical help: for clothes, food, rent money. Others sought help with personal problems or hoped she would advocate on their behalf with federal agencies. Still others wrote in to praise or criticize her many and often unconventional opinions and activities. Then there were those who were merely curious about her life as first lady and a public figure—a fascination that would endure long after she had left the White House.

Eleanor could not magically solve people's problems or make them disappear, but the fact that she responded with warmth, sympathy, and understanding established her reputation as a compassionate, thoughtful public figure who was willing to engage directly with people—an image she reinforced through her syndicated newspaper column "My Day," her weekly White House press conferences, her national lecture tours, her radio programs, and her frequent personal appearances.[3]

These efforts paid dividends. By the time she started writing "If You Ask Me" in May 1941, Eleanor had established credibility and trust with her audience. Millions of Americans had seen her, heard her on the radio, read her newspaper column. They felt they knew her, and she, in turn, felt a bond with them.

"If You Ask Me" ran first in the *Ladies Home Journal* (1941–1949) and then *McCall's* (1949–1962),* two of the most popular women's magazines in the country, with circulations of more than 6.5 million readers in 1961. The column's premise was simple: readers sent in questions, and Eleanor answered them. There was no filter and very little spin. Her answers were so candid that her editors included a disclaimer that her views were not necessarily those of the magazine or, in the column's early years, the Roosevelt administration.[4]

Initial reader reaction to "If You Ask Me" was intense, so much so that the *Ladies Home Journal* editors had to admit in print that they were "not altogether prepared" for the heavy response.†[5] By 1946,

---

* Eleanor Roosevelt moved to *McCall's* in June 1949 after a dispute with the editors of the *Ladies Home Journal* over the serialization of the second volume of her autobiography, *This I Remember*.

† In her August 1943 column, Eleanor Roosevelt reported that the *Ladies Home Journal* editors had received "hundreds of questions."

"If You Ask Me" had become so successful that Eleanor published a version of this book based on the columns to that date that also included her answers to additional questions posed by more than forty well-known Americans in government, the arts, media, science, and medicine. She published a similar collection in 1954 called *It Seems to Me*, which is also out of print.[6]

When the column began, Eleanor's husband, Franklin D. Roosevelt (F.D.R.), had begun an unprecedented third term, and Europe was at war. Americans were jittery and afraid. Many of the first columns dealt with military and home front concerns as readers sought information and reassurance. After F.D.R.'s death and the end of World War II, readers' questions revolved around the return to a peacetime economy, the Cold War, domestic political issues such as civil rights and civil liberties, and social problems such as juvenile delinquency, health care, and aging. Questions of etiquette also became more prominent, as did queries on interpersonal relationships.

As an advice columnist, Eleanor did not claim to be a psychologist, a life coach, or a fortune-teller. What she offered was advice based on her education, her life experience, her professional expertise, and, above all, her deeply held principles. By 1941, she had taught at a school, co-owned and operated a furniture-making business, and held leadership positions in the Democratic Party at the local, state, and national levels. She had worked with labor leaders and civil rights activists and been a key player in the development of New Deal programs that improved the lives of women and youth. Her subsequent travels during World War II and her postwar work at the United Nations (U.N.), particularly her role as chair of the U.N. Human Rights Commission, gave her additional expertise in foreign affairs.

She had also raised five children; lived with a difficult mother-in-law and a remote, unfaithful spouse; wrote books and magazine articles; hosted radio programs; and edited a monthly parenting magazine on babies for a middle-class audience.*[7] In addition, she was an enthusiastic reviewer of children's literature, an avid cultural consumer, and a peripatetic traveler at a time when few Americans ventured far from home.

If her readers saw her columns as a source of information, advice, and reassurance, Eleanor viewed them as another vehicle to connect with people and promote her vision of a just, open, diverse, and inclusive society. For her, democracy was "a way of life" based on "belief in the value of each individual" and a democratic society was one in which everyone had access to jobs, adequate housing, health care, and education.[8]

While acknowledging that these were ambitious goals, she nevertheless believed they were achievable given enough imagination, courage, and effort on the part of all Americans. "Each individual has to fully live up to the obligations of citizenship," she wrote in 1944. "So each of us has the obligation to know how to make our citizenship count."[9]

Eleanor deplored the fear that gripped her contemporaries, considering it the major obstacle Americans faced in creating a more perfect union and a more peaceful world. She challenged her fellow citizens to move beyond mere tolerance to full acceptance and understanding. "The problem is not to learn tolerance of your neighbors, but to see that all alike have hope and opportunity," she wrote in a 1945 article titled "Tolerance Is an Ugly Word."[10]

Above all, Eleanor believed in her country and its people. While she did not minimize the difficulties the United States faced, neither did she allow them to overwhelm her. She believed the values

---

* Between 1921 and her death in 1962, Eleanor Roosevelt wrote twenty-seven books and almost 600 articles in addition to 246 "If You Ask Me" columns and more than 8,000 "My Day" columns.

she espoused—dialogue, civility, inclusiveness, cooperation, and a healthy curiosity—would steer the country through perilous times.

What readers take from this book will of course be shaped by their own attitudes and experiences. Those concerned with political divisiveness and inequality will find meaningful, practical advice on ways to bring people together. Glass-ceiling breakers and social justice warriors will be inspired by Eleanor's perseverance against the "isms" of her time. Parents and educators will find a sympathetic colleague in their efforts to shape the young. College students and young professionals trying to navigate a complicated and often contradictory world will find a guiding hand. Aspiring politicians and leaders will learn what it takes to be effective in those roles. Teenagers itching for freedom and respect will gain a wise friend while those seeking a third act will be empowered to make the most of the time they have.

While Eleanor was certainly progressive for her era, it may be helpful to remember that the meaning of the words "progressive" and "liberal" have shifted over time. To contemporary eyes, some of her answers may seem surprising or even disappointing. It's also important to realize that these columns were never meant to be Eleanor's last word. They were written in the moment, in the language of the era, and reflect her thoughts and feelings at a particular time, and while her thinking might have evolved had she lived longer, no one can say with certainty how she would have approached contemporary problems. Eleanor herself acknowledged as much. "You can really never tell what a man who has been a thinker and a leader . . . would think or do if he were alive and facing new circumstances," she wrote shortly after F.D.R.'s death. "You can take what he has written and what he said and what you know of his character and principles, and it may influence you in your thinking. But it should never be considered as the attitude of the man in the new situation. A new decision should always be the result of new thinking."[11]

At the same time, it's also worth noting that *how* Eleanor answers a question is just as important as what she says. Her deft handling of hostile queries is a master class on how to cope with the antagonism and vitriol that pervade today's online world, while her answers to nosy questions are a five-star P.R. tutorial on the way to forge a connection with an audience while still maintaining personal boundaries.

More than fifty years have passed since Eleanor wrote "If You Ask Me." Much has changed; yet much remains the same. Although we live in an increasingly wired world where events seem to move at warp speed and every day brings a fresh controversy, we still worry about our relationships, our children's upbringing, and how to make a living. Social issues like health care and abortion are still with us, our domestic politics are fractious, and the world is no less dangerous. The questions and answers collected in these pages are a vibrant conversation between one woman and her fellow citizens about issues as relevant as the latest tweet. They remind us that even in times of tumultuous change, our essential hopes, desires, and worries remain constant. Perhaps that's why after more than half a century, her words remain so powerful.

Mary Jo Binker

TIME LINE

1884

   ஃ Eleanor Roosevelt is born on October 11 in New York City.

1892

   ஃ Eleanor Roosevelt's mother, Anna Hall Roosevelt, dies; Eleanor goes to live with her maternal grandmother, Mary Ludlow Hall.

1894

   ஃ Eleanor Roosevelt's father, Elliott Roosevelt, dies.

1899-1902

   ஃ Eleanor Roosevelt attends Allenswood School in England.

1902

   ஃ Eleanor Roosevelt returns to the United States, and makes her debut into New York society.

1903-1904

   ஃ Eleanor Roosevelt teaches dancing and calisthenics at the College Settlement House on Rivington Street and investigates sweatshops for the Consumers' League in New York City.

1905

   ⚘ Eleanor Roosevelt marries Franklin D. Roosevelt (F.D.R.) in New York City.

1906

   ⚘ The Roosevelts' daughter, Anna, is born.

1907

   ⚘ The Roosevelts' son James is born.

1909

   ⚘ The Roosevelts' son Franklin Jr. is born in March and dies in November.

1910

   ⚘ The Roosevelts' son Elliott is born.

   ⚘ F.D.R. is elected to the New York State Senate.

1913

   ⚘ F.D.R. is appointed assistant secretary of the Navy.

   ⚘ The Roosevelt family moves to Washington, D.C.

1914

   ⚘ The Roosevelts' son Franklin Jr. is born.

   ⚘ World War I begins in Europe.

1916

   ⚘ The Roosevelts' son John is born.

1917

   ⚘ The United States enters World War I.

   ⚘ Eleanor Roosevelt volunteers with the American Red Cross canteens, Navy League knitting projects, and naval hospitals.

1918

- ❧ World War I ends.
- ❧ Eleanor Roosevelt discovers F.D.R.'s relationship with her social secretary, Lucy Mercer (Rutherfurd); the Roosevelts discuss divorce but ultimately decide to remain together.

1920

- ❧ The Nineteenth Amendment is ratified and American women vote for the first time.
- ❧ F.D.R. runs unsuccessfully for the vice presidency.
- ❧ The Roosevelt family returns to New York.
- ❧ Eleanor Roosevelt joins the New York League of Women Voters.

1921

- ❧ F.D.R. contracts polio.

1922

- ❧ Eleanor Roosevelt joins the Women's Trade Union League and begins working with the Women's Division of the New York State Democratic Committee.
- ❧ She meets and befriends Democratic Party activists Marion Dickerman, Nancy Cook, and Caroline O'Day.

1923

- ❧ With her friend Esther Lape, Eleanor Roosevelt organizes and publicizes the Bok Peace Prize competition.

1924

- ❧ Eleanor Roosevelt chairs the women's platform committee at the Democratic National Convention held in New York City.

1925

   ❦ Eleanor Roosevelt becomes editor of the *Women's Democratic News*, published by the Women's Division of the New York State Democratic Committee.

   ❦ She builds Stone Cottage as a retreat with her friends Marion Dickerman and Nancy Cook at Val-Kill on the Roosevelt family's Hyde Park, New York, estate.

1927

   ❦ Eleanor Roosevelt purchases Todhunter School in New York City with Marion Dickerman and Nancy Cook, and she begins teaching courses in American history, English, and American literature.

   ❦ The three women open Val-Kill Industries, a furniture factory, to provide employment for Hyde Park residents.

1928

   ❦ Eleanor Roosevelt directs women's activities for the Democratic National Committee.

   ❦ F.D.R. is elected governor of New York; after his election, Eleanor Roosevelt resigns her political posts.

1929

   ❦ Great Depression begins.

1930

   ❦ F.D.R. is re-elected governor of New York.

1929-1932

   ❦ Eleanor Roosevelt continues teaching at Todhunter School; writes occasional articles for national magazines; and travels New York State inspecting state institutions for F.D.R.

1932

- F.D.R. is elected president.
- Eleanor Roosevelt begins a series of commercially sponsored radio commentaries.

1933

- Eleanor Roosevelt begins weekly press conferences open to women reporters only, starts traveling around the country, and begins advocating for Arthurdale, a federal resettlement community for poverty-stricken coal miners and their families in West Virginia.
- She writes *It's Up to the Women*.

1934

- Eleanor Roosevelt resumes radio broadcasting.
- She begins working with African American leaders on racial issues.
- She lobbies for federal anti-lynching legislation.

1935

- Eleanor Roosevelt helps establish the National Youth Administration
- She begins writing her syndicated newspaper column "My Day."

1936

- Eleanor Roosevelt begins making twice-yearly paid lecture tours.
- Val-Kill Industries closes.
- F.D.R. is re-elected for a second term.

1937

⚬ *This Is My Story*, the first volume of Eleanor Roosevelt's autobiography, is published; the *Ladies Home Journal* serializes the book before publication.

1938

⚬ Eleanor Roosevelt attends the first meeting of the Southern Conference for Human Welfare in Birmingham, Alabama, and defies segregation laws by sitting in the aisle between the white and African-American participants.

⚬ *This Troubled World* is published.

1939

⚬ Eleanor Roosevelt resigns from the Daughters of the American Revolution after the group refuses to allow African-American singer Marian Anderson to perform in its facility.

⚬ She attends hearings of the House Un-American Activities Committee (HUAC) to support young people called to testify about communist connections.

⚬ World War II begins in Europe.

1940

⚬ Eleanor Roosevelt gives a decisive speech to a fractious Democratic Party convention divided over the question of whether or not to support F.D.R.'s preferred vice-presidential candidate, Henry Wallace, that resolves the question and unites the party.

⚬ *The Moral Basis of Democracy* is published.

⚬ F.D.R. is elected to a third term.

1941

- ∽ "If You Ask Me" column begins in the *Ladies Home Journal*.
- ∽ Eleanor Roosevelt becomes assistant director of the Office of Civilian Defense (OCD), the first time a first lady holds an official government position.
- ∽ The Japanese attack Pearl Harbor; the United States enters Word War II.

1942

- ∽ Eleanor Roosevelt resigns from the OCD after congressional criticism of some of her plans and hires.
- ∽ She travels to England to see the British home front effort and visit American troops stationed there.

1943

- ∽ Eleanor Roosevelt travels to the South Pacific to visit servicemen and -women.

1944

- ∽ Eleanor Roosevelt visits U.S. military installations in the Caribbean and South America.
- ∽ D-Day.
- ∽ F.D.R. is elected to a fourth term.

1945

- ∽ F.D.R. dies in Warm Springs, GA; Harry S. Truman becomes president.
- ∽ World War II in Europe ends.
- ∽ The United States drops the atom bomb on Hiroshima and Nagasaki; war in the Pacific ends.
- ∽ Eleanor Roosevelt joins the board of the N.A.A.C.P.
- ∽ Harry S. Truman appoints Eleanor Roosevelt a delegate to the first meeting of the U.N. General Assembly.

1946

- Eleanor Roosevelt attends first meeting of the U.N. General Assembly in London.
- *If You Ask Me* is published.
- She is elected chair of the U.N. Human Rights Commission; begins drafting what will become the Universal Declaration of Human Rights.

1947-1948

- Eleanor Roosevelt continues work on the Universal Declaration of Human Rights.

1948

- Berlin Airlift begins after the Soviets cut off vehicular access to the city.
- Harry S. Truman is re-elected.
- The U.N. General Assembly adopts the Universal Declaration of Human Rights.

1949

- "If You Ask Me" begins appearing in *McCall's* magazine.
- *This I Remember*, the second volume of Eleanor Roosevelt's autobiography, is published.
- Soviet Union successfully detonates its first atom bomb.
- Chinese communists take control of mainland China.

1950

- Senator Joseph McCarthy (R-WI) announces in a Wheeling, West Virginia, speech that he has a list of more than two hundred communist sympathizers in the State Department.
- The Korean War begins.

1952

- Eleanor Roosevelt campaigns for Democratic presidential candidate Adlai Stevenson.
- Dwight D. Eisenhower is elected president.
- She resigns from her post at the U.N.
- She travels in the Middle East, India, and Southeast Asia.

1953

- Eleanor Roosevelt joins the American Association for the United Nations as a volunteer.
- She travels to Japan, Hong Kong, Turkey, Greece, and Yugoslavia.
- *India and the Awakening East* and the *UN Today and Tomorrow* are published.
- The Korean War ends.

1954

- *Ladies of Courage* and *It Seems to Me*, a second book based on "If You Ask Me," are published.
- The U.S. Supreme Court issues its ruling in *Brown v. Board of Education* outlawing segregation in public education.

1955

- Eleanor Roosevelt travels to Israel, Japan, Hong Kong, Indonesia, Cambodia, and the Philippines.
- The Montgomery Bus Boycott begins.

1956

- Eleanor Roosevelt campaigns for Democratic presidential candidate Adlai Stevenson.
- The Hungarian Revolution.
- The Suez Crisis.
- Dwight D. Eisenhower elected to a second term.

1957

- Eleanor Roosevelt visits the Soviet Union and Morocco, and interviews Soviet premier Nikita Khrushchev at Yalta.
- Nine African-American students attempt to enroll at Little Rock High School despite intense opposition.
- Soviets launch *Sputnik*.

1958

- Eleanor Roosevelt speaks at the Highlander Folk School despite Ku Klux Klan threats.
- She visits the Soviet Union.
- *On My Own*, the third volume of Eleanor Roosevelt's autobiography, is published.

1959

- Eleanor Roosevelt begins teaching at Brandeis University.
- Fidel Castro comes to power in Cuba.
- She testifies at a congressional hearing in support of the minimum wage.
- She travels to Israel and Iran.

1960

- Four African-American college students stage a sit-in at a Woolworth lunch counter in Greensboro, North Carolina, sparking a movement that spreads throughout the South.
- Soviets shoot down American U-2 spy plane over Russia.
- Eleanor Roosevelt campaigns for Democratic presidential nominee John F. Kennedy.
- *You Learn by Living* is published.

1961

- CIA-trained Cuban exiles launch the Bay of Pigs invasion of Cuba, which quickly fails.
- Freedom Riders protesting segregation on interstate transportation are beaten as they travel from Washington, DC, to New Orleans.
- President John F. Kennedy appoints Eleanor Roosevelt to the U.S. Delegation to the United Nations.
- *The Autobiography of Eleanor Roosevelt* and *Your Teens and Mine* are published.
- She writes *Tomorrow Is Now* and *Eleanor Roosevelt's Book of Common Sense Etiquette*.
- President John F. Kennedy appoints Eleanor Roosevelt chair of the President's Commission on the Status of Women.

1962

- Eleanor Roosevelt chairs a hearing to investigate the conduct of federal judges hearing the cases against the Freedom Riders.
- She travels to Europe and Israel.
- Cuban Missile Crisis.
- Eleanor Roosevelt dies at age seventy-eight in New York City.

Chapter 1

WOMEN AND GENDER

THE THIRTY YEARS between the election of Franklin D. Roosevelt in 1932 and Eleanor Roosevelt's death in 1962 were a study in contrasts for American women. During the Great Depression, women were often denied jobs because government policy and popular attitudes prioritized male employment. Once America entered World War II in 1941, women were deemed essential labor, and millions of them went to work in defense industries only to be fired once male veterans began returning. In the postwar period, a revived economy and the advent of an expansive consumer culture enabled many white women to enjoy a middle-class standard of living for the first time. Some used this newfound status to build lives as housewives and mothers, roles that popular culture celebrated in the Mad Men era of the 1950s and early '60s. However, many women—more than a quarter of all females in 1950—also continued to work, thus ensuring that Eleanor's column would continue to be a forum for questions about work-life balance and other issues related to women's lives.[1]

By virtue of her position, her activism, and her own experience, Eleanor could offer advice for navigating this time of social change and demolish stereotypes of "typical" female behavior. As early as 1933, she had argued, in a book titled *It's Up to the Women*, that the modern woman was a worker capable of combining a job with marriage and motherhood. In her view, a woman ought "to be able to do something which expresses her own personality even though she may be a wife and mother." She never deviated from that position. To the very end of her life, Eleanor actively encouraged women to work, enter politics, and engage with the outside world. In fact, her last official duty was to chair the President's Commission on the Status of Women, which reviewed women's progress in all sectors of American life and made recommendations for "constructive action" in such areas as employment; legislation; political, civil, and property rights; and family relations. The group's final report, issued after her death, reflected her concern for equal opportunity, equal pay, and expanded opportunities for women.[2]

Although she did not live to see the rise of the modern women's movement, Eleanor's fingerprints are all over it. The work she and her allies did between 1920 and 1962 laid the political, economic, and social groundwork that later generations would use as a launchpad for efforts such as Title IX and Hillary Clinton's presidential campaigns. Echoes of her insistence on a woman's right to make her own choices are also apparent in the "leaning in" and "having it all" movements.

While Eleanor celebrated the gains women had made and looked forward to their continued progress, she understood that the quest for equality was far from over. "The battle for the individual rights of women is one of long standing," she wrote in 1941, "and none of us should countenance anything which undermines it." In a culture where women still struggle to be heard and where issues such as pay inequality, domestic violence, and sexual harassment dominate the news cycle, that insight resonates as powerfully as her suggestion that women use the accomplishments of their forebears as an impetus to "go out and work harder."[3]

Do you think equal pay to women who fill men's jobs is economically justified?

Certainly. If women do the same work I have always believed that they should receive the same pay. [MARCH 1944]

What can be done to help saleswomen to obtain a living wage?

The only thing that can be done to help any workers to obtain proper working conditions and to get better wages is to organize. Only the strength of an organization of workers can bring about any changes. [JUNE 1944]

Which do you think is the harder—working in an office all day or doing the housework for a family?

Doing housework for a family. Usually work in the office is centered about a particular job that needs to be done, and when it is done it is over for the day. The housework for the family, however, may start when the youngest member of the family wakes up and it goes on through the vicissitudes of the day until late into the night. [NOVEMBER 1945]

Women need more time to be women, not merely cogs in the machinery of the business world. Why don't more employers use double shifts or something that will make it possible for more women to work part-time?

I am afraid if women want to be considered on a par with men in the business world they must work a man's hours and find time for their own interests in their spare time. Part-time shifts in most businesses are very difficult and not as efficient as full-time work. However, where there is a possibility of giving part-time work it should be arranged so it does not hurt the work to be done, and where women need part-time work because of home duties it should be available. [OCTOBER 1949]

It seems to me that women who hold jobs outside the home should be allowed income-tax deductions for domestic help they would not otherwise employ. What is your opinion of this?

I do not see why women who work outside the home should be allowed to deduct the cost of domestic help any more than men who employ domestic help in their homes are allowed to deduct the wages from their income tax. If a woman wants to hold a job outside of the home, she does it on exactly the same basis as a man, and should take the same deductions on her business expenses as he does. If she has help for reasons that are connected with her business, such as entertainment, she can legitimately, I imagine, show the connection and make a deduction. But what deductions she makes should be on that basis and not on the basis of "I want to work and therefore need help in my home." [MARCH 1951]

Eleanor Roosevelt's views on deductions changed particularly with regard to working mothers, who by the end of the 1950s were a third of the female workforce. Two years after she answered the question below, Eleanor described the rule against

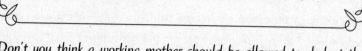

working mothers deducting the cost of a "home worker" as
"unrealistic and unfair."[4]

*Don't you think a working mother should be allowed to deduct the
salary of a housekeeper from her income tax?*

Yes, I do. The working mother must have someone to stay with
her children and to take the burden of the house from her shoulders. It is certainly a part of her business to have someone in her
house to help her, so it would seem to me a legitimate deduction
from her income tax. [MARCH 1959]

Although she had long fought for women's rights, Eleanor Roosevelt was ambivalent about the effort to ratify an Equal Rights
Amendment. Based on her experience with the women's labor
movement in the 1920s, '30s, and '40s, she believed ratification of such an amendment would adversely affect hard-won
protections for women working in industry by invalidating
protective legislation that among other things set maximum
working hours and exempted them from jobs then considered
too dangerous for them. As her answer below indicates, she believed it would be more productive to concentrate on repealing
state laws limiting women's rights and activities because "it is
usually the state laws that really affect their lives." However,
the movement of women into male-dominated trade unions
during and after World War II combined with her work with
the U.N. Human Rights Commission and the U.N.'s Commission on the Status of Women did make her rethink her position.
Still, she never fully endorsed the Equal Rights Amendment.[5]

I know that you used to be against the Equal Rights Amendment. Since its form has changed somewhat, and since various organizations have changed their minds in regard to it, I am wondering what your present opinion is. If you are now for the amendment what are your reasons?

I have always felt that the Equal Rights Amendment was unnecessary and that, if we put half the work which has to be expended on getting an amendment to the Constitution into amending the state laws which are really objectionable as they concern women in our various states, we would be better off and further ahead than we are now. I objected to the Equal Rights Amendment at first because of its effect on women in industry, particularly the unorganized women in industry. I am not sure that I think even now there is sufficient organization among the working women to make it possible to do away with all protective legislation for women. For that reason I think I would still prefer to see us give our energies to the removal from the statute books of really harmful legislation which handicaps women. However, if the majority of women in the country decide that they desire an Equal Rights Amendment of course all of us will accept it, since we all believe, in this country, in majority rule. [JUNE 1949]

Don't you think we should have a law protecting the victims of sex crimes from the publicity they receive when they report these crimes to the police?

I think there should be a law to protect anyone who does not wish to be given publicity. [JULY 1952]

Have you ever said to yourself, "If only I were a man"? Or are you quite content with being a woman?

> No, I have never wanted to be a man. I have often wanted to be more effective as a woman, but I have never felt that trousers would do the trick! [OCTOBER 1941]

Men frequently claim that women show little loyalty between themselves, have practically no sense of sex solidarity. What do you think about this?

> I do not think you can talk about sex solidarity in women any more than you can in men. Both men and women will stand up for each other at times, and both men and women are sometimes disloyal to each other, but I do not think women are apt to be any more disloyal to other women than men are to other men. It is the person and not the sex which counts. [JANUARY 1942]

Generally speaking, do you think women are less truthful than men?

> No. Women are quite as truthful as men, sometimes even more so. [JANUARY 1942]

Do you think women have as much sense of humor as men?

> A sense of humor is purely personal and has nothing to do with sex. I have known men with no sense of humor and I have known women with none. Both men and women can have a keen sense of humor and both can have none.
>
> Sometimes I think that women are more apt to have a greater sense of fun because they have traditionally adapted themselves

to the mood of the people they are with and therefore reflect the atmosphere around them more quickly than do men. [JULY 1944]

What do you think is American women's commonest fault? American men's?

I am surprised that you should even suggest that the American woman has any faults; but since you do suggest it, I think perhaps it is their inability to take criticism and use it to the best advantage. This is a fault shared by both men and women very frequently. [OCTOBER 1941]

A very intelligent man I know complains that women now spend most of this country's money, and by the end of the war they will have all the jobs and men will have no chance at all. Do you think there is any truth in this?

I think it is complete nonsense. If men go around, however, talking like that they will create a psychology which will bring about the very thing they wish to prevent. [JUNE 1942]

What do you consider the most unattractive characteristic of a woman's manner in social activities—loquaciousness, reticence, aloofness, insincere enthusiasm, cattiness, and so on?

I consider the most unattractive characteristic anyone can have, man or woman, is the kind of selfishness or lack of consideration which leads to all the other things you have mentioned. One of the very important social attributes of a woman is that she be interested in other people more than in herself. [MARCH 1945]

Since American women spend so much of their time in business and politics, what can be done to keep them out of the taverns? Do you think if taverns were licensed to sell spiritous liquors only, and if tables and chairs for women and soft drinks and all food and music were banned in taverns, it would do any good?

I haven't the faintest idea. Women nearly always go where men go. In the long run, it seems to me, the important thing is to make whatever place people go to a decent place in which to be.

[FEBRUARY 1946]

What do you consider the best years of a woman's life?

I do not really know what are the best years of a woman's life, because it depends so much on how she develops. If she is able to learn from life to get the best out of it at all times, then probably at whatever age she is those years will be the best she has had. But we do not all do that.

If you ask me what years I thought were the most enjoyable I would again have to qualify my answer because the enjoyment is different at different times. Certainly the years when women have young children are very rewarding, but again they are often filled with anxiety.

The years of youth, when there is less responsibility, are enjoyable—but the anxieties of youth are also very marked, and there are few young people who escape them.

The best thing we all can do is to learn to make use of the years as they go by and enjoy whatever period of life we are in.

[MARCH 1951]

Recently in your page in the Journal you stated your approval of women holding political office, but said you did not feel qualified yourself. What qualifications should a woman have to run for Congress?

She should be fairly young and strong and healthy. She should have a good education and if possible some experience in political work on a community and state level. She should have convictions as to what she believes is necessary for her community and for the nation as a whole, and she should have some comprehension of the nation's place in the world of today. [DECEMBER 1945]

I can't see that women have derived any benefit at all from the right to vote. Do you think they have? If so, what?

I most certainly do. The benefit they have derived, from my point of view, is the fact that they can exert their direct influence and build up tremendous power because of their vote and that of other women, which can be cast for the things they really care about. Women wield the same power over their representatives that men do, and they carry equal responsibility. I prefer to do that myself rather than rely on persuading the men I happen to know to act as I think they should. [APRIL 1951]

Do you feel there is a double standard in politics? That is, are women candidates for office treated more gently by their opponents than men?

I have watched a great many women in political life, and I think there may be more reticence in bringing up certain types of accusation against a woman. I have an idea, however, that if accusations have some foundation in fact, they won't be left out of a political campaign. When anyone, man or woman, goes into politics, I believe one has to develop a pretty tough skin and take for granted one will be treated no more gently than any other candidate. [MARCH 1962]

Chapter 2

RACE AND ETHNICITY

RACE AND ETHNICITY were seldom mentioned in the *Ladies Home Journal* or *McCall's* during the time the column appeared. Both publications were aimed at a white middle-class audience, and the questions the editors asked Eleanor Roosevelt to answer reflected that bias. Yet, given her strong public support for blacks—by the 1940s she was strongly identified with the issue of civil justice—and her activism on behalf of other minority groups, including Native Americans and Jews, it was inevitable that readers would ask Eleanor about her views.

Most of the sixty printed questions pertaining to race seemed to come from white writers. Only two readers asking race-related questions identified themselves as black. One white woman married to a Chinese man wrote to ask for advice on how to deal with insulting remarks. During World War II, two readers whose race could not be determined asked about discrimination and bias against Japanese Americans. One white veteran who had commanded black troops during the war wrote to ask about careers in "the field of race relationships."[1] Several questions came from people concerned about anti-Semitism, which was prevalent at the time. Many of the remaining queries came from white readers who were uneasy about the prospect of racial integration and what it would mean for their way of life. They were particularly concerned about the integration of schools and intermarriage. To allay these concerns, Eleanor distinguished between legal equality, which could be legislated, and social equality, which she thought would come in time.

Eleanor emphasized time and time again that civil equality was vital to the success of American democracy. Unless discrimination was eradicated, it would warp the social fabric at home and diminish American influence abroad. "If we cannot meet the challenge of fairness to our citizens of every nationality . . . then we shall have removed from the world, the one real hope for the future on which all humanity must now rely," she wrote.[2]

At the same time, Eleanor was no pie-in-the-sky idealist. She understood that some of the difficulties involved in racial and ethnic discrimination were grounded in what she called "the insecurity of some of our people under our economic system. If times are hard, jobs scarce and food hard to get, . . . we fight to keep ourselves on top," she wrote in 1946. "We come to attribute certain characteristics to different races and nationalities. . . . If they are not our own, we are apt to lump people all together as doing certain things."[3]

While she believed that equality of opportunity would help resolve many of the practical issues surrounding racism and bigotry, Eleanor knew that the core of the problem was personal and emotional. That's why her answers to readers' questions so often revolved around the individual's responsibility to eliminate racism. "Staying aloof is not a solution," she wrote at the end of her life. "It is a cowardly evasion."[4]

None of her remedies are quick or slick, but they are practical, and as relevant today as when she wrote them. Eleanor challenged her readers to examine their own beliefs, leave their comfort zones, learn to like people of different races and backgrounds, and when they encountered racism, to confront it. She also urged them to band together with other like-minded people to build public support for a more just, equal, and diverse society, believing that the weight of that pressure would do "more than any other single factor" to help eliminate racism and bigotry.[5]

What is the best thing to do when people you meet casually—say a taxicab driver or an office receptionist—make violently prejudiced (and untrue) remarks about a minority race? Usually I just keep my mouth shut. But is this really right? It seems to me that perhaps in keeping silent I am actually condoning these vicious remarks.

I rather think the time has come when keeping silent, if other people say things of which you cannot approve, is an escape from doing something disagreeable. Everyone has a right to his own opinion and to state it, therefore I do not think one should be heated or angry over what other people say; but if silence seems to give approval, then remaining silent is cowardly. I think one should say, "I have evidently had different experiences from what you have had, and I find on the whole that thus and so seems true." It may lead to an argument and it may require restraint and patience on both sides, but it will often clear up misconceptions and show that there are two points of view, and that it is possible to discuss questions on a reasonable basis even when feelings are involved as well as facts. [SEPTEMBER 1944]

What do you think the average person, white and black, can do to promote better understanding between the two races?

I think that for all of us the first and most important thing is to face ourselves and our own prejudices and decide what we feel. Next I think we should analyze whether what we feel is justified or not justified. If we feel it is not justified, either for personal or public reasons, then I think we should decide, taking into consideration our personal situation and the situation of our community, what are the ways in which we can help promote good feeling in our community. Sometimes it is unwise to move too fast. It is always wise, I think, if you feel something is wrong, to try to stand up for what you believe is right. [OCTOBER 1944]

If you're a guest in a house where a slurring remark is made about a minority group, do you protest or remain politely silent?

If I can possibly do so without being rude or making people uncomfortable, I try to pick up the remarks and reason them out. But if this cannot be done, I usually try to leave that particular house as soon as possible. [APRIL 1951]

We have been transferred to a part of the country where people do not share our "liberal" ideas about minority groups. Our child is actually being ostracized because of our mildly stated views. Do you think we should keep silent over crucial questions in order to be accepted socially, or speak up and suffer?

It depends very much, of course, on what part of the country you are in. If you live in a place where certain things are old tradition and you are a newcomer from another area, I think it is wise only to state your views when actually asked for them. If you are placed in this position it would be cowardly not to say what you think, but I would try to say it as unantagonistically as possible. Changes are coming in the world, no matter how much some people would rather not have them, but it is better that they are carried through by the people of the area and not by newcomers. I don't think I would volunteer anything about beliefs not held by my neighbors. [DECEMBER 1954]

Do you have any close personal friends, people you see a lot of, who are Negroes?

I don't see a great deal of many people. In fact, I can think of only two couples outside of my own children whom I see constantly, so I cannot say that I have that kind of intimacy with any Negro friends; but I have some warm personal friends whom I do see fairly often who are Negroes. [OCTOBER 1958]

Do you think it is possible for anyone to rid himself completely of a prejudice he has grown up with? Have you personally overcome any prejudice that may have been imposed on you in your early life?

I cannot remember ever having any racial or religious prejudice forced on me either by environment or by precept or example. As I have grown older, I have worked closely with questions where prejudice plays a very great part; but my own difficulties have rarely arisen from prejudice. They come much more frequently, I believe, from the natural tendency to like or dislike an individual. I have often found, however, that someone I disliked at first sight, I later learned to like as I came to know him well. It was lack of knowledge and understanding that created my first feeling of personal antipathy. [SEPTEMBER 1962]

Do you think that it is wise to teach children that all men are created equal?

It is wise, I think, to teach children that intrinsically every human being has the same value before his Maker, but that the moment a child enters the world he is conditioned by his surroundings and that, therefore, there is inequality of opportunity and of development. Therefore, we as individuals should always try to recognize the actual worth of a human being as such and, where opportunities have not been present, make allowances and work toward a world where every individual may have the chance to develop his abilities to the greatest possible extent. [JUNE 1941]

Do you believe that complete racial equality will ever be achieved? If so, how?

I do not know quite what you mean by complete racial equality. If you mean respect for the individual and equality as a citizen and in all social contacts; regardless of what race or creed you may belong to, I certainly expect it can be achieved, as we achieve a more perfect democracy and live up to our religious beliefs. The same God created all human beings and He certainly never intended that we should have less respect for any one of His creatures than for another. If we believe in religious teaching and in a real democracy, we shall give equal respect to human beings, and equal opportunity to live freely and participate in community life to every human being. [JULY 1941]

Do you really think all men are created equal?

Yes, but they do not always have an equal opportunity for development, either before or after birth. [NOVEMBER 1943]

I realize that no person who has accomplished as much for the good of our nation as you have could help but step on a few toes. This is where the malicious rumor I am constantly hearing must have had its origin. It is generally believed in this part of the country that you are part Negro and that is why you are taking up for them. Could you manage to let them know the truth?

Anyone who cares to look into the genealogy of the Roosevelts—and I happen to be descended from the Theodore Roosevelt side of the family—can also look into the collateral branches and can find the answer to your question. As far as I know, I have no Negro blood; but I suppose if any of us could trace our ancestry back far enough we would find that in the tribes from which we are all originally descended, all kinds of blood is mixed. It always seems quite foolish to me to begin to wonder what strains you might have beyond those you actually know about! [MARCH 1948]

Do you think that antiracial outbursts should be played up or down in the press?

I do not think anything which is news should be played up or played down. I think facts should be given, but biased stories should never be written. [APRIL 1944]

During the 1930s, anti-Semitism in America surged, fueled by the effects of the Great Depression, the rise of Nazism in Germany, and anti-immigrant sentiment at home. Some anti-Semitic activity, such as the anti-Jewish propaganda of Gerald L. K. Smith and Father Charles Coughlin, was overt; other activities, such as restrictive housing covenants, employment restrictions, and admissions quotas at universities, were subtler. Anti-Semitism continued to flourish through World War II, ebbing only after the conflict ended, and the full scope of the Holocaust was revealed.[6]

Eleanor Roosevelt, who had overcome her own earlier prejudices through her work with Jewish colleagues in the settlement house, labor, women's, and civil liberties movements, regarded the rising tide of anti-Semitism with alarm, particularly as Jews began fleeing Nazi Germany and war became increasingly likely. To her, racial prejudice and anti-Semitism were both motivated by the same emotion: fear, and fear could have devastating consequences for democracy. "When we allow one group of people to look down upon another, then we may for a short time bring hardship on some particular group of people, but . . . the real wrong is done to democracy. . . . We are then breeding people who cannot live under a democratic form of government and must be controlled by force."[7]

How do you feel about Jewish people taking Gentile names?

This is only done, I imagine, when Christian people have made them feel that there is such a prejudice against them that they will find it easier to face the world without a foreign name. It makes me very sad to think that Christian people could be so unkind. If the name is changed purely to make it easier to pronounce or to spell, and not under any compulsion, then I have no feeling about it. [MARCH 1942]

As a Jew I have often been puzzled what to answer when confronted with a request for either my nationality or my religion. Since I was born here, my nation is America, and I do not follow the doctrines of any religion. Yet I am considered deceptive by some in replying "American" to my nationality and "None" to my religion. What do you, as an American and a Christian, think my response should be, and in what manner do you consider me to be a Jew?

As I understand it, to be a Jew is to belong to the Jewish religion; the term has nothing whatever to do with a racial background. If you want to be completely honest, you would naturally say, "I am an American, born in this country. My parents [or grandparents, as the case may be] came from such and such a country. I belong to no religion, but my parents were of the Jewish faith." [AUGUST 1942]

I am of Jewish extraction and lately have begun to feel that there is a great deal of intolerance against us in this country. Every time I glance at my two babies I wonder how long it will be before the reign of terror descends upon them. Am I being unduly pessimistic?

I think you are much too pessimistic. I do not think for a moment that there will be in this country a reign of terror. There is too much recognition of the fact that there is something that needs to be fought and too many people who would feel that the whole fabric of this nation was falling apart. If such things as happened in

Germany were to begin to happen here, many of us would feel the purpose underlying the founding of our nation had been negated. [AUGUST 1946]

At a meeting at which you were the principal speaker I overheard two women who appeared to be intelligent and leaders in their own communities state that they were not prejudiced, but they just "did not like Jewish people." How can we hope for lasting peace and better understanding among peoples of the world when here at home intolerance exists among people who are trying to assume positions of leadership?

I do not think we can. Those of us who have prejudices will have to make every effort to overcome them, since the only hope for peace in the world is to understand and like people of different religions and nationalities and races. [OCTOBER 1946]

Chapter 3

POLITICS AND ECONOMICS

ALTHOUGH ELEANOR ROOSEVELT believed profoundly in the democratic form of government, she was not blind to its weaknesses. She knew that a democracy was only as viable as its citizens. "Politics is the participation of the citizen in his government," she wrote in her 1960 book, *You Learn by Living.* "The kind of government he has depends entirely on the quality of that participation."[1]

For Eleanor, political participation meant active engagement in local, state, and national affairs. It meant working at the grassroots level as she did in the 1920s when she and her colleagues organized newly enfranchised Democratic women in the state of New York to support progressive causes, including unemployment insurance, occupational safety and health legislation, pure food and milk legislation, and the right of women to serve on juries.[2] It meant personal investigation of community conditions, as she did as first lady when she toured the slum alleys of Washington, D.C., to draw attention to their dire condition. It meant standing up for the ideals she believed in as she did in 1939 when she resigned from the Daughters of the American Revolution because the group would not allow African-American opera singer Marian Anderson to sing in its auditorium.

It also meant raising money for the candidates, causes, and organizations she supported.

Above all it meant the free exchange of views with one's friends, neighbors, and associates. "It is not only important but mentally invigorating to discuss political matters with people whose opinions differ radically from one's own," she wrote. "Through discussion you can get fresh light on situations and fresh facts about conditions. Above all, you can . . . learn to test your beliefs and opinions."[3]

The questions in this chapter reveal how much—and how little—Americans' political beliefs and opinions have evolved since Eleanor wrote "If You Ask Me." Women and minorities have made great progress, but we're still arguing over the role of government, what it means to respect the nation's flag, and what businesspeople who enter government service should do with their assets. We're still worried about how to handle political disagreements among friends and frenemies, how to distinguish fact from fake news, and how to increase voter participation. Social media and search engine optimization have made learning about both sides of an issue more difficult—and less likely. The election of a female president remains a dream, and of course, the health of the economy is still a perennial concern.

Although "If You Ask Me" was written against a backdrop of rising prosperity, problems persisted. Two mild recessions in the 1950s slowed economic growth. Labor-management issues, muted somewhat during World War II, reemerged in the early postwar period as unions sought to solidify their gains and management tried to curb their influence. Then, as now, poverty remained intractable. A 1957 study revealed that nearly one in four Americans had an income below the government's poverty line. Income inequality was also an issue. Over the last twelve years of Eleanor's life (1950–1962) the upper fifth of the population received 43 percent of the total national income while the bottom fifth received just 4 percent.[4]

Clearly, improved conditions had not benefited everyone, erased memories of the Great Depression, or reduced the hostility that some readers felt toward unions. A staunch supporter of organized labor and working people in general, Eleanor believed that "real prosperity can only come when everybody prospers." At a time when increasing numbers of Americans are employed in the gig economy and the digital revolution has disrupted old patterns of production, consumption, and employment, her argument that workers, management, and government need to work together to ensure an economy that works for all Americans is both cogent and practical.[5]

Someone told me that you said recently in your column that the American people do not know how to govern themselves and need to be told. What exactly did you say?

I have absolutely no idea what I could have said in my column which gave such a peculiar impression. The only thing that I have said at various times is that, when the American people become apathetic and do not keep the control of their government in their own hands, it is bound to slip into the hands of those who make politics a profession. Therefore, because of their indifference, the American people may sometimes find themselves slaves to representatives who do not really represent them. [JUNE 1946]

What are the disadvantages, if any, of a democratic government such as ours?

One of the disadvantages is that reforms which are necessary come slowly. However, perhaps this is not entirely a disadvantage, because it arises from the fact that not just a few individuals but the great mass of the people must be educated to understand and desire reform. When that happens and the reform comes about, the support for it is on a very firm foundation which, though it may seem to some of us one of the drawbacks of democracy, is perhaps in the end a strength. It is undeniably true that a benevolent despot can quickly bring about better conditions and avoid suffering for the people as a whole, but one cannot always count on a despot being benevolent! However, the one thing I think we can count on is the slow but sure education of the people in their own interests. [FEBRUARY 1950]

Huey P. Long (D-LA) (1893–1935) was a flamboyant Louisiana politician whose populist politics, folksy rhetoric, and dictatorial governing methods made him both loved and loathed in Depression-era America. Long first came to power through his support for poor whites and his attacks on the business and governing elites in Louisiana. As governor of the state (1928–1932), he intimidated his opponents while championing a much-needed public works program and social welfare legislation. Elected to the U.S. Senate in 1932, he refused to relinquish power and continued governing the state, controlling many levers of power including the militia, the judiciary, elections, and tax assessment. By 1935, his Share Our Wealth Program, a plan to redistribute wealth by using the tax system to cap personal fortunes of the wealthy and distribute the surplus funds to the rest of the population, had made him a national figure and a potential contender for the 1936 Democratic presidential nomination. However, before he could consolidate his national following, he was assassinated in September 1935.[6]

Senator Joseph McCarthy (R-WI) (1908–1957) came to prominence in 1950 when he gave a speech alleging that the State Department employed more than two hundred communists. Although his charge was false, his use of a specific number plus his talent for publicity combined to make him a household name. Over the next several years he continued to make headlines with a series of allegations against public figures associated with the Truman and Roosevelt administrations and governmental entities such as the Voice of America and the Army Signal Corps. However, his contentious style and increasingly wild accusations, which had proved popular when the Democrats held the White House, became less appealing after the election of Republican Dwight D. Eisenhower in 1952. McCarthy's demise occurred in the spring of 1954 after his televised investigation into the U.S. Army's promotion of an alleged communist convinced many Americans that his charges were baseless and he himself was a bully. By the time his Senate colleagues censured him at the end of that year, his influence had evaporated. Eleanor Roosevelt was one of McCarthy's chief opponents.[7]

Men like Huey Long and Senator McCarthy have aroused fears of a "man on horseback" in the United States. Under what circumstances would we stand in danger of a dictatorship, and what would be the best ways for citizens to recognize the potential danger and oppose it?

Men who have the instincts for dictatorship are always a danger in any society. Free citizens must be constantly alert to preserve their liberties. In the United States, it is easy to discover a demagogue, but it sometimes requires courage to stand up immediately and say you don't agree with certain methods and certain ideas. However, if we want to preserve our liberties, we had better show that courage—it is the only way I know of to remain a free people. [NOVEMBER 1960]

The issue of the electoral college came up twice in the early postwar period. In 1950 Senator Henry Cabot Lodge (R-MA) introduced a proposal for a constitutional amendment to simplify the presidential election system by abolishing the electoral college. In its place he proposed splitting the electoral college votes among the presidential and vice-presidential candidates according to the state's popular vote rather than giving the candidates with the plurality of the popular vote all the state's electoral votes. The goal was to ensure that the electoral vote of each state would reflect the decision of the popular vote in that state. Although the measure passed in the Senate, the House of Representatives decisively defeated the measure, and it went no further.

In 1961, the issue was whether or not to allow residents of the District of Columbia to vote in presidential elections. This time the proposed Twenty-Third Amendment passed both houses of Congress and went to the states for ratification. Despite fears that the district's population (then 54 percent African American and Democratic) would favor Democratic candidates, three-fourths of the states ratified the amendment, and it became law in April 1961.[8]

Do you think the President of the United States should be elected by direct vote of the people?

Yes, on the whole, because I do not see why at the present time we need to continue the old system of the electoral college. Therefore, if I am given a chance to vote on the subject I shall vote for the direct placing of the names of the candidates for President on the ballot rather than having to vote for electors. [FEBRUARY 1950]

In your view, is the Electoral College a better reflection of the will of the people than the actual popular vote?

I have not been able to reach a clear-cut decision. It seems to me that in the Electoral College we get a balance of representation. However, I know a great many people who believe we should do away with the Electoral College, because it no longer serves the purpose for which it was intended. [APRIL 1961]

Would you vote for a Negro for President, or do you think opportunities for Negroes should be limited?

Any citizen of the United States with proper qualifications should be eligible for any public office. The person for whom one casts one's vote for any office should not be considered because of race or creed, but on his or her qualifications for the job, and his or her value as a leader of the people of the country as a whole. No one should be considered who could not command the support of a majority of the people of the country, because as a leader he could accomplish nothing constructive. [APRIL 1944]

In your opinion, is a man in his thirties too young to be President?

I doubt if any man in his early thirties has had enough experience at home and abroad to be President. The Constitution says a man must be thirty-five, and in the days when this great document was penned the men assumed responsibility at a much younger age than they do today, as a rule. At that time a young man had usually finished his education at seventeen, even if he had gone as far as was possible in the educational institutions of the day. Now many a boy is not through with his formal education until he is twenty-four or twenty-five, which would give him only a few years out in the world of affairs before he assumed the position which requires the greatest amount of background and experience to carry the greatest load of responsibility any one person carries in the world today. [JULY 1944]

How do you feel about the limitation of two terms for a President of the United States? Would you favor the law's repeal?

I have always felt that it was a good tradition for Presidents to serve only two terms, but I consider it unwise to have this written into law. The people should have the right to decide if circumstances arise where they feel it essential to re-elect a President more than once. [MARCH 1961]

General Douglas MacArthur once said he disapproved of a military man as President of the United States. How do you feel about this?

This is a generality and, like so many generalities, can be proved or disproved. For instance: A military man is accustomed to thinking out strategy and then giving the orders, and he might find it most difficult to work in a way which required constant negotiation and flexibility and adjustments not only within the nation but outside the nation. Life in the service also conditions a man to expect very different responses from his subordinates than one can expect in civilian life.

On the other hand, it might well be said that at certain points it is important to have the kind of quick and decisive action which is acquired through military training. [NOVEMBER 1952]

My ambition when I grow up is to go into politics and later on be President, and I'd like to know the requirements to be a good President?

I really cannot tell you because to be a good President you have to be a great many other things first. Perhaps it is best first to try to be a good man and later find out whether you can be a leader of men. If you can become a leader of men, then inevitably, I imagine, you will go into politics, and where you arrive in the long run will be partly a matter of character and partly luck or the will of God. [AUGUST 1956]

Would you care to make a long-range prediction and tell us who you think the Republican candidate for president will be in 1964?

There will undoubtedly be some soul searching in the Republican Party that may lead to the nomination of Mr. Rockefeller* or perhaps Mr. Goldwater.[19] Who knows? [FEBRUARY 1961]

In the past ten years have you changed your mind about the wisdom of any of your husband's policies?

No. As the years go by I see more and more clearly that my husband's policies, which were, of course, not his alone but those of his associates also, saved this country financially and socially. We still have a democracy, and we still have a capitalist economy. Unless we had

---

* Nelson Rockefeller (1908–1979) was a four-term governor of New York (1959–1973), vice president (1974–1977), and the leader of the liberal wing of the Republican Party.

† Senator Barry Goldwater (1909–1998) was a conservative Republican from Arizona who served in the U.S. Senate for eleven years before winning the 1964 Republican presidential nomination. After his defeat by Lyndon Johnson, he was re-elected to the U.S. Senate in 1969 and served until 1987.

met our problems in '33 in a satisfactory manner we might have had truly radical changes, as did many other countries. [FEBRUARY 1955]

In several books written since your husband was President you are referred to as "meddling" in government activities. As someone who loves and admires you, I'd like to hear your side of this story.

I was never conscious of meddling in government activities. I passed on inquiries, complaints and suggestions which were sent to me. Having learned since that time that even high department heads sometimes felt my interest meant they were obligated to do things they did not think they should do, I am shocked and grieved. I had always supposed they would do only what they thought right and not accept any suggestions they considered wrong. [APRIL 1954]

What characteristics do you feel are most important in the First Lady of our country?

I should say just the same characteristics that are important in anybody else—she should be herself, be kind, interested in the opportunities which the position affords her to help people and dispense White House hospitality with pleasure. [JANUARY 1952]

Shortly we will have not only a new President but also a new First Lady. What, according to your own experience, will be the most difficult problem the First Lady will face?

Living her own life as she wants to live it. There are certain things you are obliged to do as First Lady. In many ways, you are hemmed in, and you have to fight your way out if you feel you really want some life of your own. [MAY 1960]

It seems to be rather common practice for people who worked for the Government under the New Deal—their services having been to a degree in confidential capacity—to capitalize on their Government service by writing books or magazine articles. These people were compensated for their public service as they rendered it. Do you think it entirely proper and ethical now for them to divulge, for money, information that may reflect discredit on officials or agencies they once were paid to serve and protect?

I cannot think that anyone who was employed in the New Deal would write anything to discredit officials or agencies for which he once worked. I think it entirely proper for anyone who worked in any capacity to write a truthful account. It may not be entirely good, because many efforts had to be made to meet new situations, and you could not always be sure beforehand that everything would be successful. If the people who worked in these efforts write truthful accounts and show why certain things were done and what the objects were, I cannot think that there is any harm in writing what must eventually be of value to history. History must take cognizance of what was successful and what was not, and no one would expect that everything would be 100 per cent perfect. [JULY 1947]

Robert McNamara (1916–2009), secretary of defense in the Kennedy and Johnson administrations, had worked for the Ford Motor Company for fourteen years, rising to the post of company president before resigning to join the Kennedy administration in 1960.[10]

At the time of his appointment to the Cabinet, there was considerable publicity about the fact that Secretary of Defense McNamara had to sell his Ford holdings. Do you think it is necessary to penalize public servants in this way? It seems to me that if our Cabinet members can't be trusted to separate personal interests from public duty, they shouldn't be trusted in such important positions at all.

It is customary, and has been for many years, for people accepting positions in government to divest themselves of holdings in any enterprise that does business with the government. It is not a question of distrust; it is a question of influence that might stem from the mere fact that they have such holdings. Therefore, it is probably a wise decision that no one working in the government shall have a considerable interest in any company transacting business with the government. [APRIL 1961]

W. Averell Harriman (1891–1986), a Democratic businessman, government official, and a longtime friend and ally of the Roosevelt family, ran for the Democratic presidential nomination in 1952 and 1956. Eleanor Roosevelt favored former Illinois governor Adlai Stevenson in both instances, even though her son, Franklin Jr., managed Harriman's 1952 campaign. In 1956, Harriman, backed by former president Harry S. Truman, challenged Stevenson, who sought the nomination a second time despite his loss to Dwight D. Eisenhower in 1952. Eleanor Roosevelt's performance during a press conference at the 1956 Democratic National Convention was widely credited with stopping Harriman's bid and securing the nomination for Stevenson.[11]

When good personal friends take opposite sides politically, do you find it usually breaks up the friendship? I am wondering, for example, what your relation with the Averell Harrimans is now.

No. I see no reason for a friendship's being broken up because one holds different points of view on a variety of subjects. Friendship does not depend on seeing things exactly in the same way. My feelings are as warm and friendly toward Averell Harriman as they have ever been, and I hope he bears me no grudge for working for what I believed to be best for our country at this time. [JANUARY 1957]

Most of the people I know have been shocked to find out how many congressmen put their relatives on their payrolls. Wouldn't it be wise to pass a law forbidding members of Congress to hire members of their immediate families?

To have on the payroll members of one's family who are not doing the work or are not able to do the work is wrong. But to employ a member of one's family who is able to do the work and is of special service because of being a member of the family makes sense; to forbid it by law would be foolish. What should be done is to insist that there be justification for every individual on the payroll. Then there would be no padding of payrolls or hiring of inefficient or unnecessary members of the family. [JULY 1959]

Don't you think that filibustering is a rather silly, juvenile procedure for a supposedly dignified group like the Senate? Does it really accomplish anything that might not be better accomplished in a more adult way? Surely our lawmakers could find more profitable ways to spend their time than reading aloud from the telephone directory.

I have always thought that filibustering meant that the rules of the Senate were not good rules. I think there should be full and free debate, but it should be about the subject at hand and should not merely delay coming to a vote. [JUNE 1960]

Do you believe that seniority should be the sole factor determining the heads of congressional committees?

No. I think seniority should be taken into consideration, but qualifications for work to be done in a certain committee should be of paramount importance. [JUNE 1960]

Don't you feel our laws on abortion should be revised, so we can take advantage of our progress in medical science to prevent unfortunate births?

I have thought for a very long time that the medical profession should come together to discuss this question from all points of view. Obviously, it is a very difficult matter to legislate. Abuses are hard to prevent, regardless of which way the law reads, and lives are constantly endangered by unscrupulous and unethical so-called medical practitioners. I do feel, however, that some of the abuses of the present situation could surely be eliminated if the medical profession as a whole would make a careful survey, on the basis of which it could arrive at an agreement on how this problem should be handled on a national scale. [NOVEMBER 1962]

Do you feel that capital punishment should be abolished? Why?

I certainly do feel it should be abolished. I have said many times that the reason for punishment is acting as a deterrent to crime. It is fairly well proved that capital punishment has not accomplished this end. Human justice is not infallible, and perhaps as human beings, we should allow the right to life or death to be decided by the Creator. It would be better, it seems to me, to condemn people to prison for life and to stipulate that, short of new evidence, people who commit certain crimes should not have their sentences shortened. [SEPTEMBER 1960]

Don't you think that parents who sacrifice to send their children to college should be able to take these expenses off their income-tax return?

It would be very difficult to differentiate between those who make a sacrifice to send their children to college and those who send them when their incomes are adequate to do so. If this could be proved, a request might be made to the Treasury Department for a ruling, because it does seem to me to be an expense which could very well be considered deductible. [JUNE 1942]

Don't you think persons having extraordinary expenses for medical services should be allowed to deduct at least a portion of them from income when computing income for tax purposes?

I should think one should be allowed to deduct from one's income-tax return all medical expenses which are not covered by insurance. [AUGUST 1942]

Are you in favor of the bill your son* introduced in Congress to grant women their Social Security payments at 62?

Yes, though it seems to me that old-age pensions should be revised and given at the ages when people are found really to need them. Social Security should, I think, be available to all at 62 if the financial basis of the fund can be made secure. [FEBRUARY 1956]

Since citizens of the United States under 21 are considered minors and are not permitted to vote,† why are they burdened with income taxes, city taxes, etc.?

Paying taxes has nothing to do with the right to vote. It is dependent on what an individual is able to earn. If he has an income of $600 a year he is liable to the federal income tax law and to other taxes. This is purely an economic question and not a question of political rights. [JUNE 1949]

So much of the money you earn today must go back to the government in the form of income tax that I wonder you continue to work to earn more money. I know the virtue of keeping busy, but what's the use when you seem to keep less and less each year of what you earn? Don't you think our government has changed for the worse in this direction?

No. I don't think having to pay an income tax is any change for the worse. I like to work, and I think it is good for all of us. I take money, in some cases, for my work, though I do much work as a volunteer. To me it is worth-while working, even if much of the money is paid to the government. [FEBRUARY 1960]

---

*   The Roosevelts' oldest son, James (D-CA), served in Congress from 1954 to 1965.

†   The voting age was lowered from twenty-one to eighteen in 1971 following the ratification of the Twenty-Sixth Amendment to the Constitution.

On every hand you hear that our country is heading into a bad depression. Do you think this is true? What should be done to avoid it?

I do not think we need to have a bad depression, if our industrialists and economists learned their lesson in the 1930s. It cannot be prevented by greedy men. It must be prevented by men of wide and unselfish vision who see that no one group can garner unto itself great resources and leave the mass of people without their fair share. [SEPTEMBER 1949]

A hard core of some five million unemployed seems likely to continue, even if economic conditions improve. If this is the case, would you favor reinstituting some form of the old Works Projects Administration, to put these people to work, at government expense?

No. But I favor every effort's being made to keep our unemployment down to the smallest possible percentage of our population. [AUGUST 1961]

Why are you opposed to "right-to-work" legislation?

I am opposed to this legislation because it does not guarantee the "right to work," but gives the employer the right to exploit labor. While it is true that a great deal of labor is not unionized, much of it benefits from unionized labor's gains. If the "right-to-work" laws were passed, unionized labor would be so weakened that it could make no gains for any of its members or for those who are not members. [DECEMBER 1958]

Why are farmers singled out for subsidies while other businessmen— lawyers, for example—are left to shift for themselves?

Because the farmers are engaged in a basic occupation. If the farmers were not willing to continue their work the rest of us would starve. The farmers are engaged in probably the most exciting gamble that there is as a business venture. They gamble with the unpredictable whims of nature. The government, knowing that people must eat, tries to reduce the dangers which may overtake those who engage in this hazardous occupation of farming. [JULY 1949]

I should like an expression of your opinion on the issue of national health insurance. The physicians in our city are campaigning strongly against it as something which will handicap them and ultimately lead to "social- ism" and government control. I personally feel that our constitutional form of government contains enough elasticity to permit a form of na- tional health insurance which will help defray the overwhelming medical costs of our population without necessarily leading to government control of either the doctors or their patients. How do you feel about this?

I feel that national health insurance is a step in the right direction. I am not sure that we will find it the only answer to our problem, for it is a problem of giving the best possible medical care to those who need it regardless of the ability to pay. This is a question which will require experimentation and changes and adjustments before we reach a final happy solution. But if we do not do something we will arrive nowhere. Since the doctors have had a chance to make sug- gestions and the American Medical Association has come up with no wholly satisfactory solutions, I think it would be wise to get the cooperation of as many doctors as possible and see what can be ac- complished under the government's suggestions. [JUNE 1949]

Do you think providing middle-income housing should be made a municipal rather than a private-enterprise function?

Middle-income housing should be of interest to both private enterprise and to housing authorities. Naturally, government's first concern is subsidized housing and slum clearance. But if there is great need for middle-income housing that cannot be met privately, it should certainly be considered by government. [JUNE 1962]

Would you favor a law forbidding billboard advertising on public highways, the way they have in England?

Yes, I think it would add immeasurably to the beauty of our highways, and even occasionally to their safety. [OCTOBER 1953]

Do you feel that after three offenses a driver should have his operator's license revoked for life? If not, what would you suggest as an effective means of punishing habitual offenders?

No. I do not think three offenses should be punished by revoking a driver's license for life. I think there should be categories of offenses, some more serious than others, and perhaps more serious punishment could be evolved for a serious offense. [NOVEMBER 1950]

Would you be in favor of having certain holidays like Armistice Day, Decoration Day, and so forth, permanently fixed on Monday so we would have more three-day weekends?

I think this is a wonderful idea. It would probably give added pleasure to a great many people, and pleasure contributes to the health of the nation. [JULY 1957]

My husband was a victim of infantile paralysis when he was a child, and it left him slightly crippled on one side. He has the intelligence to pass the civil service exams, but due to his having had polio he is barred from taking the examinations. Don't you think the law on this should be changed? Surely if our country could be governed by a man who had it the government should accept workers who could qualify although they've had polio?

Yes, I entirely agree with you that any law which bars a man from taking an examination for the civil service when he is able to do the work that the examination entails is a very unjust law. Of course, it is necessary for the man to demonstrate that he can manage to do the work, and if he can prove this I certainly do not think that he should be barred, because of physical handicap, from participation in the work needed by the government. [JUNE 1949]

For years, there has been controversy over whether cameras should be allowed in the courtroom. Those who believe they should be feel that the public is not receiving full coverage of important court cases. Those who disagree contend that the presence of cameras would be distracting to the jury. What is your view?

My view is that there should not be any TV, radio, or cameras in courtrooms. The newspaper reporters can tell us all we need to know, and it is much more dignified and less sensational than when a court is disturbed by the inevitable flurry these other forms of communication create. [FEBRUARY 1961]

My husband says the Truman administration is a cesspool of corruption. How can I answer him?

You can tell your husband that if any government is "a cesspool of corruption" every individual citizen in the country is responsible when the government is a republic. Governments do not become corrupt unless their citizens have allowed low standards to exist. If you live in a democracy, you set the standards as the individual citizen. You elect your representatives, and the government belongs to you. You and I have to correct anything that is wrong—and we can always be heard. If anything is wrong, the blame is ours. [JULY 1951]

What do you believe accounts for the failure of so many of our American citizens to vote? Do you feel that this lethargy or indifference is simply a part of the democratic system and that we will go on making progress in spite of it? Or do you think it constitutes a real threat to our basic freedom?

I certainly do not think our failure to vote is part of our democratic system. I think it stems from the fact so many people believe that all rights and freedoms that go with democracy are going on regardless of what we do. It is not made clear to us from the time we are little children, at home and in the schools, that our duties as citizens in a democracy come before any other duties and that they will be respected by our employers. It should be made clear to employers also that the opportunity to vote must be given to all their employees. It certainly constitutes a threat to our basic freedom when citizens of a democracy neglect the most elemental of their duties—the duty to vote. [NOVEMBER 1950]

(Question from Walter Reuther,* president of the United Automobile Workers-Congress of Industrial Organizations†)[12]

I have to make a speech at school about the meaning of the flag, and I would like to know what the flag means to you.

The flag symbolizes for me the nation which we all love. When we pledge allegiance to the flag we pledge allegiance not only to our country but to the freedoms and principles which have built this nation. [JANUARY 1954]

What do you think of President Kennedy's creation of a Peace Corps, which will enlist volunteer American men and women for unpaid service in the developing countries of the world? Can it really accomplish anything?

I think the Peace Corps is a remarkably good idea, and I think it can accomplish a great deal. It is, however, a developing organization, and many things will change during its development period, so one cannot judge it now as a finished organization. In fact, it will never be a finished organization, because it must always fit into the general organization of the whole United States program abroad. [JUNE 1961]

---

* Walter Reuther (1907–1970) was an American labor leader and a close friend of Eleanor Roosevelt's.

† For a period in the 1950s, "If You Ask Me" opened with a question from a prominent American.

Do you think it's worth spending billions of dollars to beat the Russians to the moon when so many areas on earth need financial aid so desperately? Isn't it simply a shockingly expensive propaganda measure?

I don't think the President or the government would decide to spend more money on the project unless they felt it had either psychological importance or military value. I confess that, not being a scientist, I am more interested in what we can do to make our own earth a better place to live. But I realize that science cannot stand still. It may be part of the moving forward on earth for our scientists to move forward in the knowledge of the whole universe. Nothing our government does today is a purely propaganda measure, and everything it does is shockingly expensive. But progress is necessary in every field, so there is no use in our being critical unless we really understand what we are critical about. [OCTOBER 1961]

Arthur M. Schlesinger, Jr., (1917–2009) was a Harvard history professor, a liberal political activist, and a friend of Eleanor Roosevelt's. Among his books was a three-volume history of Franklin D. Roosevelt's New Deal.[13]

Arthur M. Schlesinger, Jr., special assistant to President Kennedy, was quoted as saying the welfare-state idea was deeply consistent with the American tradition. Perhaps I misunderstand the term "welfare state," but I do not think it is at all in the American tradition. Do you agree with Mr. Schlesinger's statement?

I am sorry to say I don't know the framework in which Mr. Schlesinger made his statement. I don't see anything inconsistent with our system in increasing our central government's interest in the welfare of the people in general to meet the situations that have grown up in our society. In our early days, each man was forced to look after himself and to go to the help of his neighbor, because he had to count on his neighbor to help him. However, as life has become more complex, the government has assumed more responsibility. I think it is quite in the American tradition to have the government institute measures needed for the welfare of the people. [MAY 1961]

J. Edgar Hoover said that one reason for purging homosexuals out of the State Department is that they are open to blackmail. Isn't this also true of a married man having an affair with another woman, or of any public figure whose personal life is subject to social disapproval? Why draw the line at homosexuals?

Yes. I suppose in public life any wrongdoing makes one vulnerable, as nobody wants to figure in a scandal. On the other hand, if one has the courage to acknowledge wrongdoing and makes amends as far as possible, one will find, I think, that an astonishing number of people are not so perfect themselves but they can understand and forgive others' failings and weaknesses.

I imagine the reason J. Edgar Hoover picked homosexuality is that it is thought of as an abnormality, and people are usually much harder on anything that seems to them somewhat abnormal. [APRIL 1951]

With national and world affairs being what they are today, I would like to make my opinions count. Is there any way other than writing to my congressman in which to do this?

Yes, the most potent way is talking to your neighbors and friends, and creating public opinion. Whether we live in a large or a small city, or in a village, it is what we and our neighbors think which really influences our representatives in the states and in the nation. [FEBRUARY 1947]

Although we are all urged to keep abreast of national and international problems, I find this very hard to do. When I read newspaper accounts of what's happening, I find that they never explain the background. Is there any way that the average person—without unlimited time—can get the whole story on important issues?

The best way I know to get the whole story on important events is to read the news and opinion magazines. They have both the space and the time to supply background material, while a newspaper usually can only report the most recent developments in a situation. Ideally, I think one should read two of these magazines—one with a generally liberal and one with a generally conservative point of view. [OCTOBER 1962]

Would you please try to name me a newspaper that isn't slanted politically? If you don't know one that is completely unslanted, perhaps you would tell me which you consider the least slanted. I am nineteen and will vote in the next election.

I would say that for objectivity the best newspaper is *The Christian Science Monitor*. Nearly all good metropolitan newspapers, such as *The New York Times* and the *New York Herald Tribune*, are unslanted in their news coverage. When you read editorial pages or columns, you are getting the opinions of certain individuals; and therefore you have to judge for yourself whether you agree with them or not. [MAY 1958]

What do you consider the major faults of the American press?

I would say the faults vary. I happen to live in New York, where we get very good coverage of both national and international affairs; but when I travel in other states, I find there are few papers you can count on to give the same type of news coverage. This is a real mistake, for we all need to be conscious of the world as a whole today. Occasionally, I find, news stories are colored by the wishes or interests of the owners; the reporters are not permitted to report objectively. This is bad, because, while the editorial page of a paper is permitted to reflect the individual views of the people writing it or of the owner or publisher, the news should be reported as nearly as possible without color. One other criticism I have found is perhaps the fault of the readers, as newspapers insist they try to give the readers what they want. This is the excuse for an emphasis on crimes and sensational stories. I think it would be better to leave these in the files of the police departments, rather than spreading them on the pages of our newspapers. [JULY 1961]

How complete and unbiased is our world-news coverage? Would our newspapers ever tell us if people were escaping from West Berlin into East Berlin, or report anything positive about Red China?

I think our world-news coverage is fairly complete and unbiased. I am quite sure that if there were a substantial movement of people from West Berlin to East Berlin, we would hear about it, either from our own press or from the British papers. It is very difficult for our papers to report anything correctly about Red China, because we have no representatives of the press or diplomatic service there. But unbiased news can be obtained from many travelers and from Canadian and British sources. [APRIL 1962]

What can a housewife do to equip herself with as much factual information as possible before voting in state and national elections?

She can read two newspapers that represent different points of view, and she can join an organization that will give her nonpartisan information both on candidates and issues, such as the League of Women Voters, or the Union for Democratic Action. [NOVEMBER 1946]

Is it possible for any man to rise to a high position in politics without being subject to mudslinging?

Oh, yes, I suppose it's possible, though he would have to be pretty careful about doing anything at all. The less he did that would make friends or enemies, the easier it would be to avoid mudslinging. [FEBRUARY 1960]

As a visitor to the United States I would like to ask why your people are so afraid of "intellectuals." In Europe we welcome this quality in our leaders.

I do not think we are really, any of us, afraid of intellectuals in this country. That idea, it seems to me, has been more or less manufactured by certain politicians. We do not like pretentiousness, and when people try to show off their superior wisdom I think the average American is likely to be amused rather than admiring. Real knowledge and education are admired in this country as much as in any other country. [SEPTEMBER 1956]

Why is it that so many political candidates—not infrequently, even very successful ones—seem to be badly educated, ungrammatical, and rather vulgar people? I have heard it suggested that the American people want leaders who are "no better than I am."

I cannot agree with your statement. Many of our most successful men have been highly educated. To take just Presidents: Theodore Roosevelt was one of the best-read people I have ever known. Herbert Hoover was an educated man. Woodrow Wilson was a scholar. My own husband was very widely read and highly educated. I think the American people appreciate culture and learning in their leaders. It is all nonsense that they want to have representatives, according to your quote, "no better than I am." [JULY 1962]

How much money do you spend a year in contributions to political causes?

It varies according to the years. In campaign years, of course, I may give a little more, but I would think a few hundred dollars, at most five hundred, would cover any year. [AUGUST 1954]

How much importance do you think wealth had in helping your husband up the political ladder?

My husband was never a wealthy man, particularly not in his youth, but he did have enough money so that he felt free to run for office, knowing that he could support his family modestly and would not be depending for bread and butter only on his salary. That sense of freedom may have contributed to his entering politics. I am glad that my husband did not have great wealth, however, because I feel that this is a detriment to anyone who wants to run for public office. [JULY 1957]

Do you think being a millionaire is a help or a hindrance in political life?

It is neither a help nor a hindrance. People pay very little attention to this particular factor. They look to see what a man does with his money. [MARCH 1959]

Please explain why it is that the nineteenth-century liberals fought for the liberation of the individual from the control of the state or government, while today's liberals seem to be always on the side of more government controls over the individual.

Because in the nineteenth century the individual had comparatively few liberties. There was no recognition that the government owed an individual certain things as a right. There were charities, but at that time the government was not conceived as doing away with charity. Now it is accepted that the government has an obligation to guard the rights of an individual so carefully that he never reaches a point which needs charity.

Nowadays the government controls which are advocated by the liberals are all to safeguard, in a modern and very complicated world, some of the things which individuals have come to feel they have a right to achieve. For instance, we insist that the government must see that every man who wants to work is able to get work suitable to his ability and at a wage on which he and his family can live. The nineteenth-century liberals did not have to face that problem and therefore no regulation was needed. Regulations have come only as our complicated civilization has made them necessary. [JULY 1948]

What is your definition of a liberal?

A liberal, I believe, should have an open mind. He should try to see that there are usually two sides to every question and that both must be considered before a final decision can be made. A liberal must be willing to consider new ideas and to experiment and must never condemn new things just because they are new. [JANUARY 1962]

American history has shown that our government is great because it is a two-party government with each party making its contributions and constantly prodding the opposition to put forth its best efforts. Although your sympathies are understandably allied with the Democratic Party, do you not feel that the balance of power should shift at regular intervals?

I do not know that I would feel that the balance of power had to shift at any regular intervals. I do believe strongly in the two-party system for the reasons which you give, but I think the balance of power should shift when the people feel it necessary or advisable. That does not mean that any precise time should be laid down. It has always been evident that our people shift from time to time. For instance, we had a shift toward conservatism four years ago and again two years ago which affected many congressional candidates and local situations. In the last election that trend was reversed, showing that the swing goes on fairly often and is affected by the needs of the people as they see them. [MARCH 1949]

What do you think is the most important difference in principle between the Democratic and Republican Parties today?

I think the difference is the same as it has always been. The Democrats are initiators. They are not afraid to try something new. They start new programs. Sometimes these fail, but more often they prove to be good. The programs are then taken over by the Republicans, who announce they will run them better than the Democrats have done, which is sometimes the case and sometimes not! [NOVEMBER 1961]

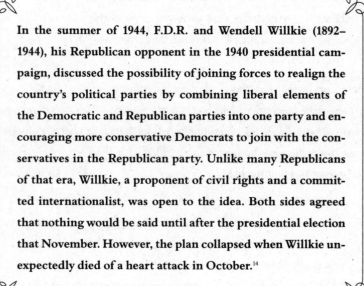

In the summer of 1944, F.D.R. and Wendell Willkie (1892–1944), his Republican opponent in the 1940 presidential campaign, discussed the possibility of joining forces to realign the country's political parties by combining liberal elements of the Democratic and Republican parties into one party and encouraging more conservative Democrats to join with the conservatives in the Republican party. Unlike many Republicans of that era, Willkie, a proponent of civil rights and a committed internationalist, was open to the idea. Both sides agreed that nothing would be said until after the presidential election that November. However, the plan collapsed when Willkie unexpectedly died of a heart attack in October.[14]

It has been suggested that since old party lines—Republican and Democratic—are disappearing and political thought is now divided between liberal and conservative groups, it would be a good idea to adopt these as the party names. Would you be in favor of such a change?

It would certainly be more realistic, but I frankly doubt that such a change will be made. I remember that my husband and Mr. Willkie discussed this possibility some years ago. But then, as now, a good many Congressmen who would lose their positions of seniority by such a change were strongly opposed. And while the public grumbles a lot on this subject, many people still prefer the traditional names, and I doubt if others care enough to bring the necessary pressure to bear. [NOVEMBER 1962]

Do you have any close friends who are Republicans?

Not only do I have Republican friends, but my youngest son and his wife are ardent Republicans! [MAY 1960]

Have you ever voted Republican?

No, I have never voted Republican because women did not have a vote prior to 1920. In 1912 I attended meetings and would have voted for Theodore Roosevelt had women been allowed to vote at that time. Since that time I have never voted for a Republican candidate because I never felt that on the whole the Republican candidate was better than the Democratic candidate. [JANUARY 1953]

If you were confronted with an inferior Democratic candidate and a really superior Republican candidate, which would you vote for, and why?

In a national or state election, I would probably vote for the Democrat. I feel that he would be surrounded by able people who would make him live up to the traditions of the Democratic Party, at least in a higher office. This does not hold true in local elections. In these elections, quite frankly, I think it is wise to vote for the individual rather than for the party. [OCTOBER 1960]

Just how far do you personally believe political-party loyalty should be carried? If you felt that President Kennedy were making some serious mistake, would you (1) volunteer your opinion to the public, (2) wait to be questioned about your feelings, or (3) simply keep silent?

I don't think that one should ever support anything one thinks is a serious mistake for the country, and I have often been critical of specific Democratic stands. If I felt strongly about something, I would certainly express my opinion in public and not keep silent or wait to be questioned. In the matter of voting—which, I suppose, is also a question of party loyalty—I do, however, consider the party as well as the man, because I know how difficult it is for a man to act independently of his party. [NOVEMBER 1961]

Although she encouraged women to be politically active and to run for elective office, Eleanor Roosevelt steadfastly refused to be a candidate herself once she left the White House. After years of supporting her husband's policies including those she disagreed with, she wanted to be free from the need to hew to an administration's or a party's line. "There is a freedom in being responsible only to yourself which I would now find it hard to surrender in taking a party office," she wrote in a 1946 *Look* magazine article, aptly titled "Why I Do Not Choose to Run." She also did not want to overshadow her sons, several of whom had political ambitions. As valid as these reasons were, they were not the whole story. Shrewd politician that she was, Eleanor knew that the time was simply not right. By the late 1950s, American women had been voting for more than thirty years, however, they had not yet achieved enough elec-

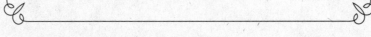

toral success at the local, state, and national levels to make her a viable presidential candidate. Moreover, she knew women were not a monolith; while some would vote for her, many, especially those who disagreed with her views on such issues as civil rights and civil liberties, would not.[15]

Are you agreeable to having a woman Vice-Presidential nominee for the Democrats?

I feel that the Vice-Presidency is not really a very wise post for women to seek as yet. I should prefer to see them in other positions where policy-making is part of their responsibility. I can understand, of course, why women voters have wanted to have a woman named for the Vice-Presidency, and I consider many women in both parties eligible for the nomination. I feel, however, that it would be wisest to seek this post when the country is ready to accept a woman as President. [MARCH 1956]

For the good of this country, wouldn't you consider running for president on the Democratic ticket? I don't think age is so important in a person with your vitality.

No. It would not be for the good of this country. It is not only a question of age. Women have not yet held enough important positions, whether elected or appointed, to attract a sufficient following for one to win the Presidency of the United States. It will be years, I think, before a woman should be elected, though I hope that eventually this will be done—not because the candidate is a woman, but because she is the person best fitted to hold the job, no matter which party she belongs to. [OCTOBER 1958]

Chapter 4

CIVIL LIBERTIES

F EAR, SUSPICION OF those who are different, campaigns to discredit government officials, alternative facts, worry over Soviet influence, concerns about privacy, and protections for free speech. These may feel like the stuff of today's headlines, but even a brief look at Eleanor Roosevelt's career reveals that, though the circumstances differed, she and her contemporaries faced many of the same core challenges.

In the late 1940s and early '50s, Americans' unease about Soviet influence in Europe and elsewhere seeped into postwar domestic politics. President Harry S. Truman's political opponents charged him with being "soft on communism" and began hunting for traitors in his administration and in the previous Roosevelt administration. In response, the Truman administration instituted loyalty oaths for federal workers, deported foreign-born communists, and prosecuted and imprisoned the leaders of the Communist Party USA. FBI surveillance of suspected radicals increased as well. The Bureau also stepped up its scrutiny of Eleanor, who already had an extensive FBI file due to her earlier association with reform organizations considered left-leaning or communist affiliated.[1]

Meanwhile, congressional committees, notably the House Un-American Activities Committee and the Senate Permanent Subcommittee on Investigations under the leadership of Senator Joseph McCarthy (R-WI), held hearings to determine the alleged communist sympathies of individuals in and out of government. In the early 1950s, Congress also passed two laws to control perceived communist subversion. The Internal Security Act required communist and "communist front" organizations to register with the federal government while the Immigration and Nationality Act allowed the government to restrict the entry of any immigrant with suspect views and deport people with ties to "subversive" organizations.

The furor over communist subversion coursed through much of U.S. society. Some Americans even began to fear their neighbors, along with many other suspect groups that often included career civil servants, activists in the labor and civil rights movements, educators, clergymen, librarians, and individuals working in the media. Suspicion could arise for little more than attending a meeting, organizing for a suspect cause, or subscribing to literature deemed subversive. In some cases, even legal activities such as speaking in support of the Bill of Rights became suspect. Individuals accused of Communist Party membership or sympathies often lost their livelihoods. Civil liberties contracted as the belief took hold that the rights of the accused could be ignored because the threat of communism was so severe.[2]

By 1953, "If You Ask Me" readers had submitted so many questions dealing with communist subversion in American life that Eleanor decided to devote an entire column to the subject—the only time she ever limited herself to a single topic.[3] Appalled at the outcry that had been created and the government's response to it, she tried to allay readers' fears, reminding them that the best way to secure America's freedom lay not in the suppression of civil liberties but in making democracy work for all its citizens. "I believe in free speech, and I am not really afraid that our people cannot be trusted to see the disadvantages of communism as long as we perfect the democratic processes at home," she wrote.[4] At the same time, she insisted dissenting views must be heard. As early as 1941, she said, "The test of democracy and civilization is to treat with fairness the individual's right to self-expression even when you can neither understand nor approve it."[5]

She also refused to countenance any abridgement of civil liberties, including censorship, telling one "If You Ask Me" reader, "I have an instinctive feeling that censorship is bad. . . . There is a difference between studying something to know and understand and refute that which is false, and inculcating a particular line for the purpose of making a convert. That is really where the line should be drawn."[6]

With nativism and xenophobia on the rise, and concerns about terrorism threaten to erode privacy protections, when questions regarding Soviet involvement in U.S. elections persist and government officials are under attack, Eleanor's refusal to give in to fear and her uncompromising support for basic American freedoms provide both an inspiration and an example.

Don't you think some control should be established by the Government over freedom of the press when this freedom is abused and used for political propaganda to the extent it is in this country? What part can the individual citizen play in achieving this control?

I am afraid if we started trying to control the press, we might really do away with an essential freedom. It is true that this freedom is often abused, but I think the basis of democracy is that we educate people sufficiently well so that they can be trusted, in the long run, to judge political propaganda and the type of news that is slanted by certain types of interests. The individual citizen can best control the press by insisting always that the papers in his own home environment write uncolored news stories. [MARCH 1947]

Do you believe that any government or religious agency should have the right to censor movies?

I happen not to like the idea of censorship, except such censorship as the people exercise when they ignore something, and personally I feel in the long run we would be better off if we relied on the industries themselves and the public to do the necessary censoring. [FEBRUARY 1953]

The question is often raised as to just how much public criticism of the United States government by its own citizens and office seekers may damage our reputation in other countries. Do you believe there is any way we can preserve our right to examine publicly the actions of our government and, at the same time, not give ammunition to powers that seek to discredit us?

The countries of the world are accustomed to the workings of our democracy. They expect Americans to criticize, and they would be surprised if we were suddenly silent. This country is too big for everyone to be always in agreement, but the world knows that in times of crisis and danger it is a unified country. Even when we think our government has been unwise, we know we must back it up if our country is in real danger. But, as long as possible, we preserve our right to try, by open discussion and criticism, to get as good a government as we can. To silence this would, I think, be a real detriment to democracy. [JANUARY 1961]

I have found out that a man and woman who are my friends are active communists. They have a store. Knowing their sympathies, I have stopped patronizing them. However, the rest of the neighborhood continue to shop there, knowing they are communists. Am I doing wrong mixing business with politics?

Communists have a right to earn a living in the United States as long as we permit them to be here. We have an obligation to allow people to think and peacefully communicate their thoughts to others as long as they do not attempt to overthrow the Government by force. For that reason the fact that people who run stores and gain a livelihood believe in certain theories which we do not believe in is no reason, from my point of view, for not associating with them. It may, however, become disagreeable to have contacts with them because you feel you are helping them to promote something in which you do not believe. In that case, you will naturally not continue your contacts. That will be for personal reasons and not because of their political views only. [JANUARY 1949]

Would it not be possible to outlaw the Communist Party in the United States, although we are supposed to be a free country where everyone can express his convictions?

I think it would be highly unwise to outlaw the Communist Party in the United States. How would you feel if you were a citizen of the U.S.S.R. and decided that you preferred to have a more democratic form of government and you were outlawed because of it? That is practically what would happen to you in Russia today, but that has never happened to us in the United States. We are a free country, we can express our convictions with only the limitation of not advocating the overthrow of the Government by force. We can use all the persuasion that lies in our power. We trust, however, that democracy will so completely meet the needs of the people that there will always be among us people who believe strongly enough in it to fight for it with words and by deeds. We must prove that the people's well-being is satisfactory because of the way we use our democracy and that there is no value in making any change. [APRIL 1949]

Up until now my husband and I have considered ourselves good Americans. Now I feel our rights as Americans are threatened because my mother and stepfather belong to the Communist party. What is to become of us and our twelve-year-old son? Will he be branded too because his grandmother is a Communist? What can we do to prove that we are good Americans?

Your situation is a difficult one, but there is, of course, no reason why you should suffer because of the ideas held by your mother and stepfather and certainly no reason why your twelve-year-old son should suffer. During the present state of mind in this country I suppose it is hard for people to think of members of a family as individuals, but it must be done. The only thing you can do is to continue to live as a good American and to insist that you do not hold communist theories and therefore should not be condemned merely by association with your mother. [DECEMBER 1949]

What is your answer to people who accuse you of being pro-Communist?

A very simple one. I have never been a Communist nor in favor of Communism at home or abroad, but I have never been afraid to come in contact with Communists, and I think it would be a poor democrat who could not stand up and meet the Communists and their theories. [MARCH 1952]

One of my grandson's professors tells his classes that the Committee on Un-American Activities is ruining our reputation in the rest of the world. First, Mrs. Roosevelt, do you think there's any truth in this? Secondly, should a man be permitted to say such things in the classroom?

Yes, I think this professor's statement is absolutely correct. As for his right to make the statement, if it is proper for an individual to hold opinions it seems to me proper for him to state them in the classroom, as long as they are not directed against the welfare of the country and do not advocate the overthrow of the government by force. [JULY 1953]

If you were asked to testify publicly about a friend who had once been a member of the Communist party but was now a loyal American, and you knew such testimony would cost him his job, what would you do?

Ordinarily if I knew a man had once been a Communist I would not hesitate to say so—and to add that I knew he was now a loyal citizen. But if I were dealing with such a hysterical situation that a statement of this kind would cost this man his chance to earn a living, and if I knew of no overriding reason for giving such testimony, I would refuse to give it. [JULY 1953]

What in your opinion is the greater danger in Communism—atheism or its economic aims?

It is very difficult to answer questions of this kind, because what I really object to most in Communism is not some of the theories—which were written by Karl Marx in an attempt to correct some of the injustices that he saw during the Industrial Revolution in England—but rather the way Communism developed under Stalin. Trying to make Stalin and the Communist party take the place of God has not succeeded even with many Russian people, and it seems to me that it would be almost impossible to wipe out religion by offering Communism in its place unless people had already lost their faith in their religion.

What I really consider the greatest danger in Communism is its creation of a police state, which puts everybody under such terror that there is no free expression of individual thinking and no dignity for the human being. The evil of Communism as it has developed in Europe is, of course, the same evil which existed in Fascism and Nazism. [SEPTEMBER 1953]

Some people think a course in Communism should be taught in our schools. How do you feel about this?

I think it would be extremely helpful to young people to understand the basis of Communism, the Party line and the Party tactics. [OCTOBER 1953]

You keep saying Americans are frightened by what's going on in this country now. Would you mind giving me a few examples of who it is that's so frightened?

I find that younger officials in government positions nowadays are extremely guarded in giving an opinion of any kind. That goes for diplomats, high and low, as well as for people in government departments. I find, too, that people will occasionally say to me that they do not want to go see So and So because they are not quite sure of what he believes in. That is an attitude one almost never encountered in the Thirties and Forties. I have also had people say they were not seeing So and So now because they were not sure of his past affiliations and that one has to be careful whom one sees. I don't know whether you call this being afraid, but I do. [APRIL 1954]

How do you feel about wire tapping? Is it justifiable when used against criminals, spies, and potential traitors?

The only time I think it is justifiable is if the authorities really know, or have reason to suspect, that they must use it to find potential spies or traitors. And then it should be done by only the most responsible authorities. Wire tapping for any other reasons whatsoever should never be allowed. [OCTOBER 1960]

Chapter 5

LOVE, MARRIAGE, AND FAMILY

QUESTIONS ABOUT LOVE, marriage, and family are the staples of any advice column, and "If You Ask Me" was no exception, especially as many midcentury Americans grappled with a number of social and demographic changes whose repercussions we're still navigating today.

Marriage rates, for example, had dipped during the Great Depression, but rose before and after World War II as young people hurried to exchange vows before shipping off to combat or married as soon as they returned. Many of these newlyweds were very young. The average age of men at first marriage dropped from 24.3 in the 1930s to 22.8 in 1950. The female age fell as well from 21.3 in the 1930s to 20.3 in 1950. These young couples also had more children—the nation's birthrate rose from fewer than twenty births per thousand in the 1930s to more than twenty-five births per thousand in 1947.[1] At the same time, birth control became more popular despite the unreliability of contraceptives and the legal and religious barriers to obtaining them. (The Food and Drug Administration did not approve "the pill" for contraceptive use until 1960, two years before Eleanor Roosevelt's death.) Abortion remained illegal, though surveys conducted under the auspices of the American Medical Association and the federal government revealed that it had been widely and clandestinely practiced in the 1930s.[2]

As marriage rates rose, so did divorce rates, reaching a high in 1946 of 43 per 1,000 people, more than double the rate at the beginning of the decade leading to uncertainty about how to deal with remarriage and blended families. The increased birth rate, the rise of a youth culture characterized by discontent and rebelliousness, and concerns about juvenile delinquency made child-rearing questions more urgent, particularly at a time when experts such as Dr. Benjamin Spock were advocating a less authoritarian style of parenting.[3]

More subtly, queries about such topics as infidelity, in-laws, division of household labor, working mothers, and disagreements over politics also reflected the stressful nature of midcentury white middle-class family life. The number of questions from female readers asking how to find partners or happiness as singletons highlighted the importance of marriage in this era as well as the perennial human desire for love and connection.

Although Eleanor had been raised to view marriage as indissoluble and homemaking and child-rearing as women's principal tasks, her own marital difficulties and need for meaningful outside work made her sympathetic to more modern concepts of marriage and child-rearing. Her openness to these ideas meant that her opinions were often at odds with those of her readers. She supported birth control at a time when it was still controversial. She favored planned parenthood as the way to reduce the number of illegal abortions. She thought that divorce, while painful and disruptive, was sometimes a couple's best option. Marriage, in her view, had to be a two-way street where neither partner was "boss" and housekeeping tasks were shared regardless of whether or not a woman worked outside the home.[4] As for raising children, she thought trust between parents and children and a nurturing family atmosphere would produce happier, better-adjusted children than one focused on discipline and rules.

As Americans continue to spend millions of dollars a year on self-help books and helicopter parents drive themselves (and their offspring) crazy in the quest to raise happy, successful children, when all it takes to meet someone is a cell phone and an app, and when marriage and childbirth are lifestyle options and same-sex marriage is legal, Eleanor's advice cuts through the noise, reminding us that successful relationships require patience, commitment, flexibility, and a healthy dose of common sense.

Do you believe in "love at first sight"?

I have heard tell of such a thing. Many people when they say "love at first sight," mean that some people have a natural attraction toward each other. This does not mean always that it will develop into the lasting love of a lifetime. [JANUARY 1944]

What, in general, is the best age to marry?

I should feel that it was a mistake to marry too early, before one's character has had an opportunity to develop, but between the ages of twenty and twenty-five seems to me good. [SEPTEMBER 1941]

I've heard it said over and over again that an intelligent young woman must make an effort to hide her intelligence if she wants to be popular with men. Do you think it is smart to act dumb?

I never think it smart to do anything which is not natural and truthful. The kind of young men who are attracted to you because you are stupid, or try to appear stupid, are not worth having around. I think every girl should make herself as attractive as possible, but I do not think she should pose and appear to know things that she really does not know. Honesty, modesty and naturalness are three very good qualities in making and keeping friends. [OCTOBER 1946]

I am a woman about forty years of age and not bad to look at, have a college education, a good responsible job, sense of humor, good disposition, and am not aggressive or set in my ways. I have never had the opportunity of

*meeting eligible, unmarried men and I am craving a home and companion-
ship. I enjoy cooking and making others happy. Have you any suggestions?*

Your situation does not sound to me very desperate. It seems to
me that at your age it ought to be possible to make opportunities for meeting eligible unmarried men. Use a little ingenuity in
your business to make friends. It is not impossible for a woman to
do some entertaining on her own, and to issue some invitations
if she becomes friendly with people whom she meets either in
the course of her work or in the course of her outside activities.
[MARCH 1949]

*Like many women in their twenties, I am beginning to face and fear a
future alone with no husband for love and companionship. What advice
would you give those of us who do not marry, to permit us to lead full
and happy lives, free of the fear of loneliness? Do you think overeduca-
tion which lifts a woman above the intellectual level of the people she
meets is ill-advised?*

I should advise any young woman who does not marry to take
a deep interest in young people, so that she will have the same
satisfaction with other children that she might have had with her
own. I should also advise her to build up very warm friendships
and cultivate her interest in some kind of work which will tie her
down to obligations, so that she will never find time hanging
heavily on her hands and feel that her existence is profitless.

There is no such thing, from my point of view, as overeduca-
tion, nor being above any people because of formal education that
you might have been fortunate enough to acquire. Anyone with
character and the opportunity can acquire a formal education,
and many people who have not had a chance for book learning

are wiser than those who have had. If education hasn't given you enough understanding so that you can get on with people around you and appreciate their quality, and perhaps help them through your opportunities to more opportunities of their own, so that their interests may coincide with yours, then I am afraid your education has done you more harm than good. [JULY 1948]

My first marriage ended very unhappily in divorce. A few years ago I met a man I thought I loved, but I was afraid to marry him for fear of repeating the first experience. We decided to live together for a while and see how things worked out. We are now happily married, but my family recently found out about our living together and won't have anything to do with us. Do you think their attitude is fair?

You are putting a difficult question up to me. Your family has, of course, a right to act as they see fit. However, it is my experience that whatever families may do temporarily, there is no way of dissolving the family tie. Your children remain your children, your brothers and sisters remain your brothers and sisters. You may not approve of one another, you may at time almost dislike one another, but there is no real happiness in breaking family ties. It is better, I think, to accept whatever comes and give and keep the love which should exist among people of the same family. [FEBRUARY 1951]

Would you advise me to tell my daughter that I met her father by way of the "Strictly Personal" column in our newspaper?

I can't imagine why you should not tell your daughter. It seems to me quite a simple matter to impart that piece of information. [JANUARY 1957]

What do you consider the three most important qualifications of a good husband?

That he shall be honest, not only in material things, but in intellectual things; that he shall be capable of real love; and that he shall find the world an increasingly interesting place in which to live every day of his life. [AUGUST 1941]

Do you think a marriage should take place between two people who are well matched in every respect except that the woman has had a better education than the man and knows more about cultural things than he does?

I see no reason why a marriage should not be entirely happy, even if the woman has had opportunities for education in certain fields which the man may lack: "Education" is a curious term. Real education is possible of achievement with comparatively few cultural advantages.

If a woman has real appreciation of the worth of her man as an individual, she will make whatever advantages she has serve his purposes. She will never make him feel in any way inferior, because she will know that fundamentally real education is knowledge that is not acquired from books alone, or from a background which has been richer in opportunity for certain kinds of culture, but depends on the ability to think clearly and to understand men and events. [JANUARY 1942]

What do you think are the most difficult problems involved in marrying an only child?

The fact that as a rule an only child has been accustomed to being the center of the stage and may find it difficult to enter into a dual relationship where each partner is equal. Also the parents of an only child are apt to expect more consideration, since their whole interest has been centered in this child, and the adjustments to the new relationship are sometimes difficult. [APRIL 1952]

I know the experts say marriage should be a 50-50 affair, but don't you honestly think most wives are happier if the husband is just slightly more the boss?

I think people are happier in marriage when neither one is the boss, but when both of them are willing to give as well as take. [SEPTEMBER 1944]

I understand you once wrote down several rules for marital happiness. Will you tell me the chief ones please?

I cannot remember ever having indulged in this pastime, but if you heard that I did so perhaps I did. I must have been more rash than I am now, so I will not try to write down more than one or two suggestions, certainly not rules.

In all human relationships, and marriage is one of the most difficult, I think perhaps the important qualities for all individuals are unselfishness and flexibility. Tact can be a help also, and real love which occasionally carries you beyond interest in yourself is essential. [NOVEMBER 1952]

When interests conflict, do you think a woman's first obligation is to her husband or to her children?

I think a woman's obligation is always to her husband. But if she is a wise woman, she will make her children feel that they, too, have an obligation to their father. Then there will be no conflicts, because they will be one family with mutual interests all of them respect. [OCTOBER 1959]

I love and admire my wife, but there is one subject on which we can never agree. She thinks I should help with the dishes. Do you think this is a husband's work?

I think anything connected with the home is as much the husband's work as the wife's. This silly idea that there is a division in housework seems to me foolish, when very often the wife earns money outside the home as well as the husband. Certainly if there are children, the wife has two jobs—the one of being a mother and the other of being a wife. The kind of man who thinks that helping with the dishes is beneath him will also think that helping with the baby is beneath him, and then he certainly is not going to be a very successful father. [JANUARY 1945]

Eleanor Roosevelt's attitude toward infidelity stemmed in part from her own experience. During World War I, F.D.R. had a romance with her social secretary, Lucy Mercer. After Eleanor discovered the relationship, the Roosevelts discussed divorce but decided against it for personal and political reasons. Although they agreed never to see each other again, F.D.R. and Lucy stayed in touch and met occasionally after she married. Toward the end of his life, she visited him in the White House on several occasions without Eleanor's knowledge. Lucy was also with F.D.R. when he died in April 1945.[5]

My husband says he has a right to have an affair with another woman when he's overseas. When I ask him if I have the same kind of rights he says no, I'm the mother of children and have to be respectable. It's not that I want an affair with another man, but I don't think his attitude is right. Do you?

Of course what your husband is trying to guard against is the feeling of guilt which comes to any man who has been physically unfaithful to the woman whom he really loves and does not want to lose. The act of being physically unfaithful seems much less important to the average man, and he finds it hard to understand why the woman he loves looks upon it as all-important. Yet, as you prove by your question to him, if a woman tries to take the same point of view a husband is quite horrified and turns to the old code of respectability on the woman's part for the sake of the children. How about respectability on the man's part being of value to the children?

There is something more, however, that should be said on this whole question, since physical faithfulness is perhaps more difficult for men than for women. I imagine your husband, who apparently does love you, is trying to make sure that you will not turn away from him if anything of the kind should happen while he is overseas. You and he will have to decide what is the right attitude to take. Nobody else can decide it for you. [JANUARY 1952]

Do you think that venereal-disease programs over the air and in the movies would help prevent the spread of this disease?

Yes, I do. Ignorance has a great deal to do with the spread of all social diseases. The only difficulty is that anything which goes over the air or is shown in the movies may be heard and seen by people for whom it is really not intended. Many children would not be able to understand certain information and should not obtain it in this way. How these vehicles for public information can be limited so they will reach only the proper groups is a question that is difficult to decide, but I think in some way we must resolve it, because the power of education controlled by the movies and the radio is too great to give up using it for this particular purpose. [AUGUST 1944]

What would you suggest to a person whose spouse is cold, taciturn and prone to belittling?

I would suggest some plain talks. If there is love between you, you may find out what is the trouble and be able to remedy the situation, although it will probably take an effort on the part of both people. [JUNE 1957]

What is your attitude toward divorce? Do you consider it advisable or moral?

Divorce is something which should never be taken lightly, but I think the real emphasis should be laid upon the seriousness with which we undertake marriage in the first place. Sometimes even when a marriage begins with every apparent prospect of success, however, people develop differently and find themselves, over a period of years, unable to live in harmony with the person to whom they are married. When that happens it seems to me that there is nothing to do but to resort to a divorce.

Certain religions do not recognize divorce, and of course I am not talking about people who belong to those religions, but it is a rare thing that people who find themselves unhappy together can have a home where there is an atmosphere of kindness and consideration and unity, which is the only atmosphere in which children can develop successfully. It is better, I think, to make the inevitable adjustment and separate, hoping that both people involved may find companionship and love with someone else, or that one can make of life alone something worth living. For two people to live unhappily together seems to me bad for them and for the children involved, if there are any. [OCTOBER 1943]

Do you believe in planned parenthood?

Yes, I do, if it is not used as an excuse to shirk having a family. I believe that every married couple should have children if they are able to do so, but I believe that they should use intelligence so that the children will be healthy and the mother not physically exhausted. Of course, if this is against your religious belief, that is a different matter, but outside of that it would seem sensible to plan intelligently for the family health and happiness. [JULY 1944]

Are you for or against birth control?

There are vast areas of the world where unless there is birth control there can be no progress. I am for birth control, particularly in places having severe problems of overpopulation and insufficient food. I can quite understand, however, that there are reasons why certain people do not believe in birth control, and I feel that people should be allowed their own decisions in this matter. [SEPTEMBER 1958]

A prominent doctor has suggested that one way to reduce the shocking abortion racket in this country would be to make prospective illegitimacy a legal cause for abortion. What do you think?

It seems to me that making prospective illegitimacy a legal cause for abortion would not in any way meet this situation. The only real answer to this question, I think, is more knowledge of planned parenthood. It is not a question which can be legislated. [MAY 1942]

What do you think could be done to cut down the great number of abortions in this country?

For married people, planned parenthood is the obvious answer. For the unmarried ones, I think if young people were brought up to have strong characters and to resist certain temptations it would help. [DECEMBER 1944]

How many children do you think make up the ideal size family?

As many as a mother and father really want. [JUNE 1941]

I have read a lot lately about artificial insemination from anonymous donors. In childless marriages, if both husband and wife want children, do you feel there are any moral or social obstacles involved?

I really know very little about this question, but I should think if both husband and wife had consented to this type of treatment, it was a question for them to decide and also of no interest to others, and should not be known to anyone but themselves and the doctor. [AUGUST 1946]

Apart from actual poverty, do you think couples should refrain from having children because they cannot give them "advantages"?

Certainly not. I do feel that the most important thing for children is to have a home which can provide them with the necessities for healthful living, with love and an example of ethical living. [JULY 1941]

In your opinion, is voluntary childlessness a bar to successful marriage?

I think that very few marriages are entirely happy if people voluntarily give up having children. Children are both a joy and a responsibility. They bring both pleasure and sorrow into the lives of their parents, but they are a tangible expression of the real love that exists between man and wife; and if you could have children and deliberately avoided it, I think something would be missing in the marriage relationship between young people. [AUGUST 1945]

Did you have any of your children the natural-childbirth way? What do you think about the theory that you should try not to use anesthetics during childbirth?

When my children were born there was very little said about the "natural" way. They were all born in my own home. The nurse gave me an anesthetic, but I can remember each child's first cry, so perhaps it wasn't too different from what they now call natural childbirth. I do not think it is a question for you to decide, however, since your doctor will use an anesthetic if he thinks it necessary when the time comes. [MAY 1952]

Do you feel having an "only child" is unfair—to the child? If it were impossible to have more than one, would you advise the adoption of a sister or brother?

I think if it is possible to have more than one child, it is better for the child you have. So many things are learned naturally when children grow up together which have to be taught with considerable difficulty if a child lives largely with grownups. If, however, it is impossible to have a brother or a sister, the question of adoption is again something which no one can advise about. Each situation is different. No child should be adopted unless it can receive the same love and care as you give your own child. Only two people who have thought it over carefully can decide whether this would be the case or not. [AUGUST 1945]

Do you believe it is pampering children for the average mother to take them to and from school by car?

No. I think if children can walk to school without danger, it is probably good for them; but if there is a good reason for taking them by car, I see no reason why it should not be done. It is a matter of common sense, and children are the first to recognize valid reasons, however, to walk. [JANUARY 1942]

How old were your children when they stopped believing in Santa Claus? What did you tell them at the time?

I do not remember the exact age when my children stopped believing in Santa Claus. What I told them was that of course there was a Santa Claus. He might not actually come down the chimney, nor perhaps have a sleigh drawn by reindeer, but I explained that in every home where the parents tried to give their children a happy time at this season of the year there was a Santa Claus. The old stories and legends were to be read and enjoyed and, if possible, preserved because they told of the different ideas and customs that had existed in many parts of the world. [DECEMBER 1951]

My sister died recently, leaving her nine-year-old daughter in my care. I know you went through something like this yourself as a child, and thought you might suggest ways my husband and I could make this little girl happy. And mistakes we might avoid.

The great thing, I think, is to make children feel that they are needed and actually belong in the family. Give them certain responsibilities, and they will respond with confidence and joy. If this child is sensitive, avoid talking about her before other people and letting her overhear your remarks about what you are doing for her. The main thing is to love her and let her give you her love. [OCTOBER 1952]

Do you approve of children's calling their parents by their first names?

I don't see that it makes the slightest difference if they and their parents prefer this arrangement. The point is what kind of relationship is built between them, not what they call each other. [APRIL 1960]

Did you ever exercise censorship over the books your children read or the movies they attended?

No, not exactly censorship, though I gave the children the books I felt would be appropriate for them to read and they would enjoy. Movies were not a problem, because, during their childhoods, films were much less an accepted diversion, and we lived mostly in the country, where we had to plan to see a movie or play. Actually, I think censorship over books is foolish, because anything harmful will probably be above children's heads and they will not take it in. They will absorb only what they are able to understand.
[NOVEMBER 1960]

Even though you are a grandmother, do you still feel responsible for the behavior of your children?

No. I feel that when one's children are grown they must assume responsibility for their own actions. The parents have done all they could by precept and example. They may suffer if they do not agree with their children, or they may recognize with pride if the children go beyond what they felt their own capacities might have led them to do, but I think all human beings have a right to assume their own responsibilities and make their own decisions, and we have no right, as elders, to interfere in their lives.
[APRIL 1945]

Do you think that mothers with professional training should try to keep on their careers, and do you think part-time jobs for women after the war would make this possible?

Every mother has to decide the question for herself. Whether she keeps on with her work, whatever it may be, or devotes a certain number of years exclusively to her family, or however she arranges it, the decision is a personal one.

Women with professional training or special skills have been so much needed during the war that they have had to give up their personal desires and go back to work; but when the war is over, it becomes again a personal choice and one which cannot be decided by anyone but the individuals involved. Part-time jobs might be good solutions for some people, and might not be for others. It all depends upon the kind of person you are and what you decide to do with your life. [SEPTEMBER 1944]

Do you think that young children get the right kind of loving care when they are left at a nursery while their mother works? The mother I am thinking of is the wife of a soldier.

If a mother is gifted in taking care of her child it is certainly preferable to be at home with it. There are many mothers, however, who are not well adapted to the constant care of children and who would rather work, for part of the time at least.

In the case you mentioned, I should say that it is not probably entirely a question of choice. The wife of a soldier might very well need the extra money which she can make by working. She might feel that working will keep her mind more occupied and will give her a feeling that she is of more value to her husband and therefore will help her through the difficult time of separation and anxiety.

A child in a well-run day nursery gets good care, and I do not think would suffer as long as the mother was with it the rest of the twenty-four hours. [MARCH 1945]

It has been estimated that 15,000,000 women will be earning their living by 1950. In your opinion, should industry and the community encourage and underwrite nursery schools for the children of working mothers?

Very decidedly. I think it is absolutely vital for the good of future generations that nursery schools be made available to care for the children of working mothers during the entire day. The next generation will seriously suffer from both the physical and mental standpoints if this is not done. [APRIL 1946]

What do you think of the idea of government-run nurseries to take care of the children of working mothers who can't afford help at home?

I think, on the whole, that instead of having government-run nurseries it is better to have cooperative nurseries where parents arrange to pay some small amount and have a say in how the nursery is run. If these nurseries need a subsidy, it should come from local organizations or government. [JUNE 1955]

Do you think that the fact that you were a "working mother" had a bad effect on your children?

I am afraid I can't claim ever to have been a working mother when my children were small. I even did very little of the usual serving on boards, and so forth. Most of my working time began when my children were much older. My really steady work can hardly be said to have begun until my youngest child was able to go to school, so I can't judge what bad effects a working mother would have on her children. [DECEMBER 1956]

My husband died three months ago. Although I am only twenty-nine, I have no intention of remarrying. My husband and I loved children, but were unfortunate enough not to have been blessed with any. I would like to adopt a little girl four or five years old. I am making my home with my parents and a younger brother who will go to college soon. I have corresponded with a chaplain in an orphanage who says he may be able to arrange for me to adopt a child. In adopting her I would take away from her the chance of being adopted by "parents." Do you think I could be both a father and mother to her and not feel I was cheating her? Financially I am more than capable of taking care of her.

Not knowing you, it is very hard for me to tell whether you could be both father and mother to your little adopted daughter, but if you care enough about her to adopt her I am sure you will make every effort to fill her life with the kind of affection and companionship which would make her feel that she had both parents. You are only twenty-nine and even if you do not intend to remarry, none of us knows what the future may hold; and if you adopt a little girl and give her the best that you have to give, someday you may find that you will want to give her a father. In any case, your young brother who will soon be going to college will furnish her with the kind of male companionship which is valuable for any youngster. [JANUARY 1949]

What do you think is the most serious mistake parents make with their children?

Children are human beings, and each is unique. What is a mistake with one may not be with another. Parents must study each child and meet his individual needs as best as they can. Perhaps what all of us need in our relationships with children is a clearer memory of our own childhoods. [AUGUST 1962]

If you knew that your children had been going through periods of unhappiness and felt that they suffered because of mistakes in your previous upbringing of them, how would you meet the thought? With what philosophy would you accept your share of the blame for suffering you would like to wipe out or alleviate but were unable to? How should a mother meet such thoughts?

I rarely have known children who, at some time in life, did not feel that they were made unhappy because of the type of upbringing that they received. As children grow older, they often realize themselves that their home had nothing to do with the unhappiness that may come to them. Perhaps you brought them unhappiness by the effort to prepare them for life. All parents, I think, feel that they haven't always been wise and that they are in some way responsible if their children suffer later on because of traits of character which might have been obliterated when they were young. The only way I think that parents can meet that is to accept the fact that no human being is all-wise; no human being always lives up to the best that he is capable of, all the time. Failures come to all people. It is sad if they affect those whom we love, but all we can do is to be very humble and, as we gain wisdom, try to help all those who suffer and show our children where we made our mistakes. [MARCH 1947]

My sister eats her heart out about mistakes she made bringing up her oldest boy. She thinks you're a great woman, Mrs. Roosevelt, and I wish you could tell her a few mistakes you think you made when your children were growing up.

I don't think any mother is ever satisfied with the way she brought up her children. She always sees her mistakes. For instance, I gave in and allowed one of my sons to be sent to boarding school, when I knew he should have been allowed to follow his own bent and stay at home, but I did not have the courage to fight against the family tradition, nor did I trust my own judgment at that time. It was a serious mistake on my part.

I made my children do a great many things as little children by way of upholding discipline from nurses and governesses, none of which I would do now. I did too little for my three older children personally when they were babies.

One can always see the mistakes made afterward, but sometimes our children will accuse us of making mistakes which we feel sure we never made. I doubt whether children ever think they have had a perfect childhood or that their parents were ideal, no matter how much the parents try to do right according to their understanding. [APRIL 1954]

It is extremely unpopular today to suggest that children owe their parents any gratitude. Don't you think everyone has an obligation to his mother and father?

I think it should be unpopular. I don't think children owe their parents any gratitude. If parents do not have enough to live on, I think that any children who love them will certainly, if able, feel the desire to give whatever they can to make their parents' lives happier. They would be strange people indeed if they did not have this feeling, and there would be something wrong with their relationship. But if children give help purely from a sense of obligation, it will be bitterly given and bitterly received. I think every human being has an obligation to all those who love him to reach the highest qualifications and achievements he possibly can to serve however he can the good of all human beings. In that way, he gives those who love him the greatest satisfaction. But it is love, not obligation, that brings about warm and happy relations within families. [FEBRUARY 1960]

Do you ever miss your children so much you wish you could cancel all your engagements and go visit them the way most mothers can do?

I think I probably see as much of my children as most mothers do. They all live in the East now except James, and he is in Congress and I see him from time to time. I have always had the theory that too long visits by the older generation with the younger, except where it is an economic necessity, were not very wise, and I would not like to pay long visits to any of my children. Seeing them frequently for short visits and knowing they are well and happy is something on which I count and without that I should certainly be unhappy. [MARCH 1956]

Do you think the shocking increase in juvenile delinquency in America is the fault of the home or the community?

There are many reasons. In some cases it may be the fault of the home; but homes make up communities, and so, in a larger sense, it is the community which fails its young people. The need for women to work outside of the home may have left young people with less home supervision, but this supervision could have been supplied if the communities had seen fit to organize themselves.

Schools might have had more supervised recreation out-of-doors; there might have been more craftwork offered in out-of-school hours. Schools might have been open in the evenings and the communities might have shared the responsibility for holding supervised parties where young people, either in the military services or in war work of some kind, could let off steam and have a good time.

In addition, the communities might have made it more possible for women who had to go to work to run their homes more efficiently and have more leisure time in that home. We have done nothing about a universal program throughout the nation for a hot school lunch for every child, for hot meals in every factory at low prices; for cheap restaurants, such as are run in Great Britain, in which people of moderate means—whole families—can be accommodated for about what it would cost for a meal at home.

Shopping has never been organized in a way to make it easy for women workers; laundry work and care of little children have never been thought through so as to make the whole setup as easy as possible and keep the home running as smoothly as possible, with the mother still in charge when she is home, and not driven to the limit of her strength by the difficulty of doing things which must be done to keep the home functioning.

It is not enough to leave this simply to the plants involved. Every plant has different problems, and they must be taken up in consultation with the workers. Sometimes mothers might want little children taken care of in the plant; but if they have long trips to and from work in crowded public conveyances, it would be better for them and the children if the day nursery could be near their homes. This same thing has to be taken into consideration where shopping is concerned. Just establishing chain stores in the plants may not meet a woman's needs, since carrying quantities of packages, with the present difficulties of transportation at hours when shifts are changing in big factories, will not be an easy task.

The exhaustion of a mother is bound to be a contributing factor to juvenile delinquency, so we really have the problem of home organization—which is largely a community problem—and I do not think we can simply say that the increase in juvenile delinquency is the fault of the home, the school or any other particular situation. The whole community setup has to be taken into consideration, and the whole community has to take its share of the responsibility for the present situation. [JANUARY 1944]

Today it is popular to blame all the problems and misbehavior of young people on broken homes. Do you believe divorce is solely or largely responsible for juvenile delinquency?

Divorce certainly is not solely responsible for juvenile delinquency. There are many other considerations. A happy, united home is obviously the best place for a child to grow up; but often, even in happy homes, there have been failures in the upbringing of children—sometimes because of lack of discipline or lack of understanding of a particular child's needs. I think if a father and mother can stay together happily, even though they may have to make certain compromises, it is better for the child. But a child is not better off if the home is going to be an unhappy one. [NOVEMBER 1959]

What do you think of the Canadian plan for subsidizing families? Would you favor legislation in this country to provide monthly payments to families of low income or to families of all incomes to help bear the cost of raising families? Do you think income deductions for children should be increased?

If a country is particularly anxious to increase the birth rate, subsidizing large families would seem to be a wise plan. However, I think it would be much better to approach the question from a different angle; namely, to put a floor under earnings and try to see that no family earned less than was consistent with a fair standard of living. Of course I realize that some people will live better on a certain amount than others, but that is a question very largely of education. It might be possible to increase income-tax deductions for children, but that, I think, should be the same for rich and poor alike. [JANUARY 1947]

My husband is stubborn as a mule about lending our children money once they get married. Reading somewhere that F.D.R. felt likewise, I'm writing to ask, did you ever help your children out without his knowing?

Never. [JANUARY 1956]

Do you think young people should marry before they are self-supporting?

Frankly, I think this depends entirely on the resources of the parents. I see no harm in a well-to-do family's contributing to the support of a young couple whose marriage they approve. On the other hand, if supporting a marriage constitutes any hardship, I am all against it. [NOVEMBER 1962]

What do you do about home gatherings with your ex-in-laws? Do they all love you? Ours evidently do not, and we are in a quandary, for we would like to see our grandchildren.

I have always made every effort to stay on friendly terms with our grandchildren's parents and their relatives. Sometimes, even when a break comes between two people, if you have loved not only your own child but the other person involved, it is possible to understand what has happened. In that case you can continue a fairly close relationship. Sometimes this may not be possible, but with courtesy and consideration and a real desire to be on friendly terms I think an arrangement can be made whereby the children in the family can grow up with affection for the relatives on both sides of the family. [MARCH 1945]

My son and his wife are Republicans, but my daughter recently married a man who favors the Democrats. No matter how hard I try I can't keep the two couples from getting into nasty political arguments. It ruins all their visits with me. Tell me, please, how do you handle political differences in your family?

I try to make them amusing. We have vast differences in our family. All of them love to argue. They can argue passionately about things they do not care about, and anyone who did not know them would think they were about to kill one another. But I find a little laughter and teasing and, if necessary, arbitrarily changing the subject make our family gatherings rather entertaining. [NOVEMBER 1952]

So many women seem to have trouble with their mothers-in-law. Do you think it is an especially difficult relationship?

A great many difficulties seem to arise in this particular relationship. Some of the problem is perhaps possessiveness on the part of the mother or the wife; some of it is lack of tact on the husband's part. There should be realization on the mother's part that she has to make a new friend and have a desire to make life easy for her son. [JULY 1959]

Do you think it possible for two mature women—mother-in-law and daughter-in-law, for instance—to live under one roof in peaceful co-existence?

I think it possible but not probable. [JULY 1961]

Have you ever been tempted to interfere in the training of your grandchildren?

Never. [JULY 1941]

I marry a widower. The first thing I see when I enter my new home is the picture of his first wife prominently displayed on the mantelpiece. He still goes to the cemetery to mourn her, carrying flowers, especially on days meaningful to his first marriage. What is the sensible attitude for each of us to display?

When you married a widower you knew he had had a first wife. In all probability you hoped that he had loved his first wife, because the fact that he had been able to love her would make it probable that he would love you.

The fact that he is still loyal to her memory and still mourns her is something you should be happy about. If you had known her you probably would join with him in thinking of her. As long as you had not known her you cannot do that, but you can at least respect and admire him for his loyalty and realize that in a different way he will give you more just because of this loyalty.

No one loves two people in exactly the same way, but one may love two people equally and yet differently. And if you love one person very much you will love another person perhaps even more because you have learned how to love and what love can mean.

Be happy with your husband in the kind of love he gives you and be grateful for his loyalty to the past, because it augurs well for his loyalty to the present. [OCTOBER 1949]

I am a widow of forty. While my husband was alive we were very happy. I loved him very much, but feel I am too young to spend the rest of my life alone. I am a working woman, so have an opportunity to meet new people every day. How much time do you think should elapse before I can decently be seen with other men?

Heavens above! You can decently be seen with other men whenever you feel like going out again. This is your life, not someone else's, and your own feeling is what is important, not what the rest of the world says. I never can understand why one cannot live one's life as one thinks is right. You can get rid of your neighbors, but you cannot get rid of yourself, so you are the person to be satisfied, not your neighbors. [NOVEMBER 1946]

Have you any words of advice or comfort for a woman who has just been widowed?

Yes. I would urge her to keep very busy, to work at something as hard as she possibly can, and to become interested in as many things and as many people as possible. To lose someone one loves and to be alone is very difficult, but this adjustment has to be made by many people, and I think it is easier if you are occupied.

[MAY 1960]

I will be twelve August 3rd. Three years ago my mother's father died. As you know, my grandmother is a "widow." My mother says some widows are happy. What is your opinion? I always talk about my grandfather because he was good and I loved him. Do you think this is all right?

Of course it is right to talk about your grandfather. Remembering people whom we have loved and who have died is an important part of our lives, and it will make your grandmother happy.

Your mother, when she says your grandmother is happy, probably means that your grandmother has learned that happiness comes from within. It is not always the outside world which makes us happy or unhappy. We can be content if we have learned to be at peace with ourselves and accept life and the will of God.

[JULY 1955]

Is it true that you lost a child in infancy? I ask because my daughter just lost her first-born baby. If you had such a tragedy, Mrs. Roosevelt, I am wondering what helped you most to get over it.

We lost our third child, who was named Franklin, at eight months from a heart ailment which came, we thought, from flu.

I think it is harder to bear when you have no other children; the loss of your first baby is a real tragedy. It happened to my brother and his wife and also to my youngest son and his wife. The disappointment is great and the only consolation is that, having had one baby, there will probably be more; but nothing can really ease the heartache except time, and faith in the wisdom and love of God. [SEPTEMBER 1955]

Chapter 6

RELIGION AND FAITH

MANY MID-TWENTIETH-CENTURY Americans placed great value on religious faith and religious institutions. Between 1940 and 1960, church membership more than doubled, surging from 64 million to 144 million. Some of this growth aligned with broader societal patterns. For Americans moving into new suburban enclaves, churches often provided a way to make friends and put down roots. In the confrontational atmosphere of the Cold War, religious engagement also offered a way to assert the superiority of democracy over "atheistic" communism. The U.S. Congress's 1954 decision to add the phrases "under God" to the pledge of allegiance and "In God We Trust" to the country's coinage suggested a link between religion and patriotism.[1]

Given the importance that many Americans attached to matters of faith, it was inevitable that readers would want to know Eleanor Roosevelt's views on such issues as the Bible, prayer, miracles, and church attendance. They also wanted to know what she thought about cremation, the existence of God, the probability of life after death, and the best way to handle interfaith marriages—issues that still perplex twenty-first-century Americans. Then, as now, readers were concerned about the role of religion in American culture and what it meant to be one nation under God in a country where church and state are separate and citizens are free to worship or not as they see fit.

Eleanor's answers reflected her own nondogmatic approach. To her, religious belief was an individual matter. A lifelong Episcopalian, she believed in regular church attendance and church activity as expressions of inner growth. If others could reach that point with or without faith, that was their decision. Ultimately, what mattered to her was "the religious teaching that we cannot live for ourselves alone, and that as long as we are here on this earth, we are all of us brothers, regardless of race, creed or color."[2]

The American religious landscape has changed greatly since Eleanor wrote those words. The United States has become more diverse religiously even as the number of Americans who profess a faith has declined. Conflicts over social issues such as birth control, abortion, and alternative lifestyles have become political as well as religious issues.

What hasn't changed is the relevance of Eleanor's call for mutual understanding and acceptance. She reminds us of our common humanity, our heritage of religious freedom, and the importance of treating one another with respect and compassion.

Do you think an avowed atheist should be allowed to teach in a university?

I think one's religion and beliefs, or lack of belief, is one's own concern. I do not think that one should impose these beliefs on one's students, but that is something for internal arrangement between the teacher and the head of the faculty, and certainly there should be no rule which bars anyone from teaching because of his religious beliefs or nonbelief. [MAY 1953]

There seems to be a trend now in public schools to start the day by saying the Lord's Prayer. Do you think this a proper thing to do, especially in classes that have children of other faiths?

The Lord's Prayer can be said by a great many children, and I see no reason why in a public school the day should not be started by saying the Lord's Prayer, as long as there is no compulsion on any child of another faith to take part in these exercises against his will. [NOVEMBER 1957]

There was a great stir in England not long ago because in a radio debate a woman gave some talks in favor of atheism. Would you be for or against letting an atheist express his views over the air here?

I would not have the slightest desire to prevent an atheist from airing his or her views. I would feel, however, that equal time should be given to anyone else who wished to protest or answer these views. There are atheists in the world, and preventing them from saying what they think is certainly not going to wipe out atheism. [MAY 1955]

I am a nineteen-year-old member of a Protestant church. But I'm not sure there is a God. My parents ask me to go to church with them, so I do; but I feel like a hypocrite. I can't talk to my mother and father, because they expect me to accept God without question. Mrs. Roosevelt, does God live, here or anywhere?

There is nothing peculiar about your anxieties. Almost all young people go through a period when they have such misgivings. There was a time when people thought of God as an individual, much like the people they knew. Today, I think many of us think of Him as a Spirit, a great Force. There is much we cannot understand; but we know that, without some help far beyond our own strength, we could never meet the needs of the world in which we live. You may never be able to decide exactly what you believe, but you can pray to and believe in a God Whose infinite wisdom allows freedom of thought and action, and Who gives hope that there will be a future and that it will be good. [APRIL 1960]

I have heard psychiatrists say that the Bible does not have adequate answers for man's problems today, and that it should be rewritten to eliminate confusion arising from outmoded theories. Do you think the Bible is out-of-date?

No, I do not think the Bible is out-of-date. It still seems to me a remarkably wise book and very satisfying to read both as to form and content. [APRIL 1947]

A preacher here in South Carolina told us you once said the Bible was just a bunch of fairy tales. I don't believe you said this, Mrs. Roosevelt, but would you mind telling me what you do think the Bible is?

I do not remember ever saying that the Bible was just a bunch of fairy tales. In fact, I know I never said it. I think I may have said that there are parts of the Old Testament which as a child I was taught to take literally and now I assess some of these as having other than literal meanings. I think the Bible is one of the most valuable and beautiful books that was ever written, and I think the more we study it the more we understand and find new meanings in it. The New Testament, especially, seems to me inspired and easier for us to understand than the Old Testament. However, I find them both very rewarding reading, and, like many other people, I have found that to read even a few verses every day is a very helpful habit. [JULY 1952]

Do you believe in a life after death? If so, how do you envision it?

I do believe that life goes on after death, but I am not sure in what way, and I do not think that important. It would seem to me wasteful if nothing came of the efforts which we make here, and I cannot believe that this is true. But the exact way in which our efforts help, or go into the future, seems impossible to know, and perhaps, therefore, we should not spend too much time wondering about it. [JUNE 1951]

My husband says he wanted to be cremated when he dies. I cannot bear the thought. It seems so unnatural. Please tell me how you feel on the subject.

I cannot see why it seems unnatural, unless it is forbidden by one's religion. All of us eventually turn to dust and ashes, whether we are buried or cremated and have our ashes put wherever we specify. It looks to me as though it will become more and more difficult to find land for cemeteries that are going to be needed by our increasing populations. In India people are burned on a funeral pyre, and I think cremation may well become a practice everywhere in the world. Personally I would feel it is quite a natural feeling on the part of your husband. [MARCH 1952]

Don't you think that people frequently use religion as an escape from something which they do not understand or will not accept? To me, the person who professes he is highly religious and attends church, but who leads a life entirely opposing these religious teachings, is far worse than the one who claims no religion.

I think everyone will agree with your statement. As to your question, I doubt very much whether anyone can long use religion as an escape. They may use it for a time to deceive themselves and others, but if they are really religious they are bound to find in their religion a challenge which has to be met in their daily lives. If it is just an assumed attitude, it will not serve you long, nor fool other people long. If you are truly religious, you must believe in certain things, and those beliefs have to be translated into action; and whether other people know it or not, you will soon be conscious of your own shortcomings and religion will cease to be an escape under those circumstances and become a constant prick to your conscience. [JULY 1945]

Religion teaches us to live by the Ten Commandments and the Golden Rule. Yet this is impossible—and impractical if you have to work for a living. Don't you think we are kidding ourselves when we say we do live by them? Wouldn't it be more honest and better for us and the people with whom we come into contact if we worked out an ethical code which it would be possible to attain?

It is a very sad commentary on our society that many people would say as you do, that they cannot earn a living and really live with their neighbors according to the Golden Rule and the Ten Commandments. I have heard it many times, and recognize the fact that in order to keep a job you will sometimes have to make compromises. Make them as little as you can, and in your own life try to live in the way that you really feel you want to live. It will change even the business conditions under which you struggle at present. No ethical code will meet the situation any better than the old religious code. It is simply that not enough people have come together with the firm determination to really live the things which they say they believe. [OCTOBER 1947]

Anybody who knows anything about you knows that you are a religious woman in the most decent and humble Protestant tradition. Can you explain why certain people seem to go out of their way to try to prove that you are not religious?

I think it is probably because I do not always explain carefully enough what I mean when I say certain things. I take it for granted that people know I have certain beliefs, traditions and standards, and I fail to repeat that these exist, since I feel they are so much a part of myself that they do not need any explanation. However, I cannot blame people for having felt that I did not explain thoroughly, and each time I make a mistake like this I promise myself not to do it again—and then I find I am very apt to do the same thing! [MAY 1952]

Do you manage to set aside any time each day so you can be by your-self and meditate?

Yes, at night. [SEPTEMBER 1953]

To what person do you turn for help when you have a deep spiritual problem?

I don't think I turn to anyone. One must face things oneself. I have, of course, one or two friends with whom I talk things over occasionally, but if it is a personal decision of a spiritual nature I don't see how anyone could make it for one. This is a case where one must pray for guidance but decide for oneself. [MAY 1954]

Were you always a religious person, or did you go through the unbe-lieving period so many people do when young? I would like to know also what experiences strengthened your religious feeling most.

I don't think I ever went through an "unbelieving" period, but as I have grown older I have found certain interpretations given by different religions interesting to study, and while I was taught by my grandmother that every word in the Bible is literally true I have as time went on considered some of it to be more or less allegoric.

I think suffering strengthens anyone's religion, because there is a feeling that one needs strength beyond one's own capacity to carry a burden, whether it be a physical, mental or spiritual bur-den. [AUGUST 1954]

Has anything ever happened to you that shook your faith in God even for a moment?

No. [MARCH 1956]

What standards do you use to judge a man's character when you know he doesn't believe in God?

I doubt that anyone does not really believe in God. People may think they don't have any belief, but you will usually find that somewhere down in a human being's soul there is a belief in something beyond himself. In any case, I would not judge a man's character by his belief or unbelief. I would judge his character by his deeds; and no matter what he said about his beliefs, his behavior would soon show whether he was a man of good character or bad. [AUGUST 1956]

When you pray, do you ever ask for specific things for yourself or others?

Not that I can remember. One's prayers, I think, are usually for guidance and strength, both when one prays for oneself and those that one loves. It would seem incongruous to pray for some specific thing. [OCTOBER 1956]

Why are you a Protestant?

I am a Protestant because I was born and brought up one and have always been satisfied in my religion. [MARCH 1957]

Has there ever been an occasion in your life when you have been helped by a sense of Divine guidance or guidance outside yourself? If so, could you say what the circumstances were?

I am sorry to say that I have never been able to feel that I was important enough to receive any kind of special guidance, but I am fairly sure that my husband felt that he had special guidance when he had difficult decisions to make. Most of us cannot feel that the decisions we have to make in everyday life are important enough to hope for a sense of special guidance. [JUNE 1958]

Do you go to church regularly? Do you engage in private prayer? Have you found prayer a solace? Do you ever have the feeling that all religion is a sham?

I will begin with your last question. I have never had the feeling that all religion is a sham. I go to my church in Hyde Park absolutely regularly when I am home. I belong to no other church and do not go regularly in other places, for the simple reason that it is not an easy thing to do. I think there are very few people in the world who do not pray, and while I do not consider prayer a solace, I think prayer is an essential to most human beings. [JUNE 1961]

Do you think it necessary to kneel when you pray?

I think it often is conducive to more concentration if you kneel when you pray, but I do not think it at all essential. Some of the most heartfelt prayers have been offered while men and women were doing some very active work. [FEBRUARY 1946]

Do you think it's possible to be a good Christian without being a regular churchgoer?

Of course it is possible to be a good Christian without being a regular churchgoer. Nevertheless, going to church has two considerations in its favor. One is the personal satisfaction and benefit derived from the services; the other is the value of the example in the community which shows that a citizen is a Christian. There is value in showing publicly where one's allegiance lies. [FEBRUARY 1952]

A short time ago my husband died very suddenly. I feel a great need for faith. But when I pray it seems to me I am just mouthing words. I must find strength. Can you tell me where you found it when your husband died?

I think if you keep on praying you will find that strength will finally come. Pray for strength to meet whatever situation you must meet in life, and the act of faith often produces remarkable results. [NOVEMBER 1951]

Do you think people of different religions should marry if parents object?

I think this is a very personal question and only the two people concerned can decide. Some married people adhere to different religions and still live happily together all their lives. Others find that a difference in religion becomes a bone of contention and one or the other member of the family usually gives in. I really think that parents who take it upon themselves to object so much that they attempt to keep the young people from marrying, are assuming a heavy burden of responsibility. Parents may not think a difference in religion is conducive to happiness, but religion is personal and only the individuals themselves can decide such a weighty matter. [MARCH 1942]

My husband and I are Jewish. Our six-year-old daughter tells us she wants to go to the Baptist Sunday School, where most of her friends go, and not to the synagogue. Do you think it would be right to send her to a school of a different faith?

The question you have asked me is a very difficult one to answer, because I do not know what the feeling of your own church would be. If she were my child, I should try to let her go on alternate Sundays to my own church and the church she wants to attend with her little friends. In that way perhaps she would get a slightly different conception of the details of both rituals. But in the case of the Jews and the Baptists there are perhaps more fundamental differences, and it might be very confusing to the child. I think this is something you will have to talk over with the child and decide in the light of your own religious beliefs. [MAY 1951]

I find that people's ideas of religion vary so greatly that I think you ought to define what is religion.

I do not know that there is any real reason why I should define what religion is. That has been done by many people far better qualified to do so. I can only give my own personal definition, which has no foundation in theology. Religion to me is simply the conviction that all human beings must hold some belief in a Power greater than themselves, and that whatever their religious belief may be, it must move them to live better in this world and to approach whatever the future holds with serenity. [OCTOBER 1941]

Do you think religion should be made a more dominant part of American life? How?

Yes, I think religion should be made a dominant part of American life, but there is only one way in which I think it can be made more dominant and that is by bringing it out of the church and into the lives led by religious people.

I read a sermon not long ago preached by an Episcopalian clergyman which might have been preached by any Christian, because he said that the most revolutionary doctrine in the world was the way of life preached by Christ Himself. Almost any other religion, if you lived up to the ideals of the founders, would lead you to what might be termed a revolutionary way of living. No political revolutions would be necessary if religion became a vital part of everyday life. [JUNE 1941]

What do you think might cause an increased church attendance?

Determination on the part of the church people to live their religion and not to leave it behind when they leave the church. Determination on the part of the church to meet honestly the problems of human beings. [SEPTEMBER 1941]

Chapter 7

ETIQUETTE

For much of the early twentieth century women's magazines such as the *Ladies Home Journal* and *McCall's* were arbiters of etiquette and good manners. The political, economic, and social changes of the 1940s, '50s, and '60s reinforced this trend with the magazines offering their white middle-class audiences behavioral advice and guidelines to navigate a variety of social situations, particularly those that socially mobile readers and their families might encounter. At the same time, the editors of these publications recognized and deplored the increasing casualness of American social behavior. In 1957, the editors of the *Ladies Home Journal* convened a panel of "writers, wits and practical observers of life" to discuss this trend and in the resulting article affirm their belief in the continued utility of good manners.[1]

Right from the get-go readers of "If You Ask Me" were concerned about questions of etiquette and proper behavior. Early queries, such as whether or not "girls should let the bars down and speak to soldiers and sailors they have not been properly introduced to," gave way to queries about when, if ever, it was acceptable to tell a white lie and whether a married woman should continue to use her maiden name.[2]

After more than thirty years in public life, including twelve as first lady, Eleanor Roosevelt was well-equipped to advise on questions of etiquette, protocol, and good manners. She even wrote a book, *Eleanor Roosevelt's Book of Common Sense Etiquette*, on the topic. For her, all the rules and conventions of polite behavior boiled down to one simple quality: kindness. "If you really act toward people in your home and out of it with kindness you will never go far wrong," she wrote. To her "the greatest courtesy" was the "warmth of friendliness" based on "sincere goodwill."[3]

In today's hyper-aggressive society when "the warmth of friendliness" and "sincere goodwill" are often in short supply, particularly in public spaces; when shouting and tweeting are considered meaningful conversation; and when the rules of polite behavior have given way to a "whatever" attitude toward almost everybody and everything, it may be useful to remember Eleanor's observation that good manners are based on the understanding that "dealing with people is never a one-way process. It must always be a matter of give and take."[4]

I find myself more and more exasperated with the way salespeople, taxi drivers, waitresses and others automatically address everyone as "honey," "dear," "sister," and the like, and in general show no courtesy to the people they are serving. To my knowledge this does not happen in other countries. Why should it be so frequent here? (It is frequent, Mrs. Roosevelt, even though you yourself may not have met with it.)

I don't think this kind of address is meant as a discourtesy. It is simply a manner of speech. I am always rather pleased when people call me by my first name, as they sometimes do in the streets or in the shops, because I know that as a rule it is a term of affection rather than a lack of courtesy. I myself would always speak to an older woman I did not know well as "Miss" or "Mrs.," but I feel sure that saying "honey" or "dear" is more a habit people have fallen into than intentional rudeness. [AUGUST 1957]

Do you feel that the trend toward overcasualness in American habits of dress, living, etc., is deplorable?

I consider it a mistake when behavior or appearance attracts attention. For instance, young people should be clean and neat and modestly dressed. They do not have to wear uncomfortable garments, but their clothes should be suitable for what they are doing. This holds true for people of all ages. As far as casualness in living goes, I think that can be extremely trying. It means that, among family and friends, you do not observe the rules of politeness and consideration of others—a great inconvenience to everyone. [OCTOBER 1960]

I'm certain that a great and gracious lady like yourself is almost never thoughtless or tactless. But if you realize that you may have unintentionally slighted someone or hurt his feelings, is it better to make a point of apologizing or better to let the incident be forgotten?

There are times when I would quite frankly say that I realized I had hurt someone's feelings, that I had not done so intentionally, and regretted it. But for the most part, an indirect approach—not forgetting the incident, but showing in subtle ways that no hurt was intended—may be better than the direct way. [AUGUST 1959]

My family laughs when I use big words or when I eat in style. Do you suggest I keep practicing good manners to myself or keep on practicing before my family? I am 11 years old.

I don't know just what you mean by "eating in style." Good manners are very simple and I am sure your family would not laugh at you if you always practiced good manners. You say "please" and "thank you"; you eat slowly but not too slowly; you watch other people and are helpful in meeting their needs. You do not take too much of anything; you eat quietly; you put your knife and fork together on the plate when you have finished eating; you don't interrupt other people who are speaking during a meal; you listen respectfully and are nevertheless responsive if anyone speaks to you. Beyond that, I can think of very little that is required of either a child or grownup in the way of table manners, and "eating in style" is something I know nothing about. [APRIL 1956]

Please explain to me why it is so terrible to write a letter to a person and not sign your name. Sometimes we wish people to know something, and what is the difference who tells them, and why do they have to know from whom it comes?

When you want to tell someone something you should be willing to stand by what you have written and to sign your name to it. No one who hasn't the courage to be identified with what he writes should indulge himself in writing. Very few people pay any attention to anonymous letters, and no one has much respect for those who write them. [DECEMBER 1947]

Have you ever been self-conscious? I am so ill-at-ease in the presence of company that I make everyone uncomfortable. I've tried to overcome this feeling, but it gets worse as I grow older. Is there any hope for me?

I have been self-conscious many, many times, and I am even today. There is only one way of overcoming self-consciousness, and that is to be so much more interested in other people around you and the things they are doing that you forget yourself. There is hope for anyone who really wants to forget herself, and I feel sure that if you can become interested enough in what other people are saying and doing, your self-consciousness will disappear. [NOVEMBER 1945]

Suppose you were to find yourself beside a complete stranger at dinner with no conversational clues to follow. How would you begin talking?

I think I would begin by asking him what he was interested in. [OCTOBER 1941]

Have you any particular way of memorizing names—or do you forget them?

I have no way of memorizing names. I often forget them, but I do my best when I hear them to connect them in some way with the face of the person whom I have met. I happen, however, to be deaf in one ear and very often I do not hear the names of people when I am introduced to them, and therefore I concentrate on remembering faces. [JANUARY 1943]

What do you do when you're talking to someone whose name you have forgotten?

I try to find out from the conversation what he or she is interested in, and sooner or later that suggests who the person is. If I cannot find out and I am not sure of finding out afterward, I usually end by frankly saying, "My memory has grown poorer with age and I remember your face very well, but I just cannot recall your name." [FEBRUARY 1945]

I need to discipline my speech and don't know exactly how to go about it. I often say something quite innocently that offends the person with whom I am talking. For instance, I mentioned someone's being fat to a fat lady. My face was as red as hers when I realized what I had done. I am thirty-nine years old and feel that I should have been able to overcome this fault long ago. What would you suggest?

I haven't any idea, my dear lady. Many of us say thoughtless things, but if they are not meant unkindly they will not be taken seriously by those to whom they are said. I think the only thing you can do is to practice thoughtfulness, and then perhaps you will speak more slowly and think first. As a matter of fact, it is really impossible never to say things which come naturally into the conversation, even if they do seem to allude to some individual in the group. [FEBRUARY 1948]

Do you think a friend of several years' standing should feel free to drop in unannounced and bring friends with her whenever she feels like it?

I think it is the right of every individual to give his friends whatever privileges he wishes them to have. One creates the rules by which one lives with one's friends. If you have a relationship in which a friend feels free to drop in unannounced and bring friends, then I should think it quite all right for a friend to do so. If, however, you do not like it, that is something you should explain, because such intimacy grows, and it grows by mutual consent. If it is disagreeable to you it will eventually end your friendship. [JANUARY 1950]

Do you feel you know a great deal about someone from the way he shakes hands? What kind of handshake makes the best impression on you, and what the worst?

Yes, I think a handshake can tell a great deal. A firm handclasp is warm and reassuring. Clammy, limp handshakes always make me think of the description of Uriah Heep, and I am never drawn to the person who greets me that way. [OCTOBER 1951]

How can I tell young guests to be more considerate of my furniture without hurting their feelings?

I think you can do it if you do it lightly and with a certain amount of amusement. You can tease youngsters about not knowing how to be careful of things which you like to have treated with consideration. I have learned, however, that as long as one has young people around it is well not to have too many things that are easily injured. [MARCH 1953]

We have neighbors whose son returned from Korea a double-amputee. Before he went to war we just exchanged casual "hellos." Now when I see him and his mother I don't know what to say to them. My feelings are so strong about his sacrifice, but words just don't come—and, besides, I'm afraid I might hurt his feelings. I'd like so much to know what you'd do in a situation like this.

I can quite understand how difficult it is for you to make openings to talk with your neighbors when such a great sacrifice has been made by this young man. If I were you I would try to be perfectly matter of fact, go on just as though nothing had happened. Both the boy and his mother want to resume life in a normal way. Before long he will probably have to go to a hospital to have artificial legs fitted. When that happens there will be plenty to talk about, because trying to learn to use them is very uncomfortable at first. But, whatever you do, remember he is still a boy, liking things he has always liked, having many of the same feelings that he had before. If you establish a normal, natural relationship with both the boy and his mother you will find soon you will be talking about everything with great ease, and even sometimes forgetting the tragedy. [APRIL 1953]

I am at a loss to know how to sign a greeting card or small gift to a lady I admire who was the wife of my son and is now married to another person.

It is a little difficult, for anyone who does not know your personal relationship with your former daughter-in-law, to suggest the way you should sign a greeting card. If your affection for her has not changed, why not express it and sign your name either as you did before, or as you would to anyone outside of your own family with whom you are on friendly terms? [JUNE 1948]

My daughter-in-law calls me by my first name. Has this ever happened to you, and do you think I have a right to ask her to call me "Mother"?

No, I do not think any of my daughters-in-law ever used my first name. Some of them call me "Mrs. Roosevelt" or "Mrs. R." The question of whether your daughter-in-law should call you "Mother" is complicated, of course, if her own mother is living. In that case, if she has a mother, she probably would not want to call you that. I called my mother-in-law "Mama," though my mother had been dead for years.

I do not think I would mind if my daughter-in-law called me by my first name, however, because it would mean that she had a warm and friendly feeling, and that, after all, is the important thing. [DECEMBER 1951]

Several of my female in-laws are unpredictably vulgar in their conversation and have caused me intense embarrassment. Am I justified in deciding to exclude them from future social gatherings at our home?

Wouldn't you hurt your wife's feelings by excluding her relatives from social gatherings? Perhaps you are a little too easily embarrassed. It might be better to pay no attention to remarks which you object to and try to guide the conversation along lines that are less objectionable. [MAY 1953]

It seems to me that there is a very fine line between what is called tactfulness and what is out-and-out deceit. How do you distinguish between them?

I suppose what you mean is that if one refrains from saying things sometimes it is almost tantamount to allowing people to form an erroneous impression. I think there are times when it is necessary to state one's opinions and then tact has to be laid aside, but there are many occasions when it does no harm to be silent, and perhaps avoid a disagreeable situation. If directly asked a question I would think it was deceit not to tell the truth. [JANUARY 1945]

Have you ever told a "white lie"? Do you think that white lies are ever justifiable?

If what you mean by a "white lie" is such pleasant things as one says casually in social relationships—for instance, saying to someone when you meet that it is a pleasure to see them, when you really have no idea whether it is going to be a pleasure or not, or telling people when you refuse an invitation that you are refusing because of a previous engagement when you are not willing to give the real reason—I certainly have told white lies and I do think they are justified. [OCTOBER 1946]

How do you get out of accepting invitations you don't want to accept? Do you permit yourself white lies occasionally?

Usually I do not have to indulge in white lies, though I might permit myself to do so. I think it is simpler to say what is true—that I have reached the limit of the commitments which I can take. Otherwise I usually try to do what I have been asked to do. [MARCH 1959]

Do you approve of married women using their maiden names? Would you have done this if your maiden name had not been Roosevelt?

I do not think it is a question of approval, it is a question of what you prefer to do. If you have made your name as a business-woman you may want to continue to use that name for business purposes. I was not in business and I have never had a career, so I would no doubt have used my husband's name. I much prefer now to be called "Mrs. Franklin D. Roosevelt," but this is purely a matter of personal taste. [FEBRUARY 1955]

In my day it was considered a sign of very poor breeding to call people by their first names unless you were close friends. Does all this first-name calling that goes on today offend you as much as it offends me?

No. It doesn't offend me at all. It is just a change in custom. Because of my age most people find it difficult to call me anything but "Mrs. Roosevelt," and sometimes I must say I am a little grieved at the formality that seems to surround me. I have become accustomed to hearing many people called by their first names and I do it myself frequently. [JULY 1955]

All the etiquette books say a widow should continue to use her husband's name. I notice that the newspapers always call you "Mrs. Eleanor Roosevelt" instead of "Mrs. Franklin D. Roosevelt." Is this because you prefer to use your own first name?

No. I much prefer Mrs. Franklin D. Roosevelt, but it seems many people find it easier to say Mrs. Eleanor Roosevelt. [JULY 1959]

My mother-in-law says that in her day it was not considered good etiquette to put intimate family photographs in the living room. I told her I'd abide by your decision in the matter, not hers, so I'd be grateful to know what you think.

I am quite sure that your mother-in-law is correct, though my mother-in-law always had photographs of the family in her living room in New York City and in Hyde Park. I never gave it a thought as to whether it was etiquette or not. I like to have photographs of my family around in all of my rooms, and so I am afraid I have just gone ahead and put them there and never really thought that it was a question with which etiquette concerned itself. [JANUARY 1952]

I have always wondered what was the right thing to do when introduced to the President of the United States. Do you just extend your hand or do you wait for him? Is it all right to call him "Mr."?

I think most Presidents hold out their hand immediately at an introduction so you will not have to hesitate. They know quite well that almost every individual is a little shy when meeting the President of the United States, and they are eager to put the person at his ease. You address the President as "Mr. President," and when you do not want to repeat it you say "Sir." [JANUARY 1957]

Are former Presidents and their wives asked back to the White House on state occasions or are they dropped like hot potatoes?

I think there is a custom which dictates the occasions on which former Presidents and their wives are formally invited to the White House. They do not automatically attend every function, because it is very difficult for the White House to accommodate all the people who have to be invited during the social season. On an informal basis there are, of course, frequent occasions when a President may want to talk to or see a former President, or when he and his wife may be invited in an entirely informal way if a personal relationship exists between them, but that is an entirely personal thing.

I will tell you a secret: by the time you have been in the White

House for one term or more, formal functions become something you go through frequently with more of a sense of duty than a pleasure. You are glad to see people, but seeing them in that formal way is not very satisfactory and it is very tiring, so I doubt if Chief Executives or their wives pine to return to the White House for formal functions. [OCTOBER 1947]

Chapter 8

YOUTH, POPULAR CULTURE, AND EDUCATION

I N THE 1940S, '50s, and early '60s, rebellious teens, anxious parents, and people convinced that the country was going to the dogs had one thing in common: they all wrote Eleanor Roosevelt. Teenagers in particular frequently sought her out. Part of her appeal to them lay in the fact that she remembered what it was to like to be shy and self-conscious. By sharing her memories of how she overcame her own awkward youth, she gave the young hope that they too could learn to be self-assured and confident. Convinced that she had been "suppressed" by "too many rules" in her own childhood and adolescence, Eleanor also sympathized with young people's desires for fewer constraints and more freedom at a time when rock and roll, tight jeans worn low, and ducktail haircuts epitomized teenage rebellion.[1] Eleanor was sympathetic to the young but never permissive. She advocated for them while consistently upholding parental authority, which made her someone parents felt they could trust.

Readers also picked her brain on all aspects of pop culture, including dating (and "necking"), dress, popularity, sex education, and the wisdom of letting boys play football. Some sought her endorsement while others hoped she would agree with their pet peeves and dire predictions about the adverse effects of a culture that offered large doses of escapism and diversion through radio, movies, and television. Eleanor's responses to these questions were always evenhanded and never doctrinaire. She thought comic books "should be carefully chosen," singing radio commercials were "no reflection on the intelligence of the American people," and television had great potential as an educational tool.

An early and enthusiastic adopter of the new medium, she hosted public affairs programs and made many guest appearances on both news and entertainment programs. She even made a controversial television commercial endorsing a brand of margarine to make money for her favorite charities. By the time of her death, she had moved into educational television where she hosted a monthly public affairs program called *Prospects of Mankind*, which featured roundtable discussions of domestic and foreign policy issues with journalists such as Edward R. Murrow and newsmakers such as John F. Kennedy, Adlai Stevenson, Nelson Rockefeller, and Henry Kissinger.[2] As a public figure in an emerging celebrity-oriented culture, Eleanor also responded to many questions from readers curious about every aspect of her personal life, from how much she spent on clothes to how much sleep she got and how she coped with fame. Although she could have sidestepped many of these queries, she seldom did because she believed that "anyone has a right to ask whatever he feels inclined to ask" and she had an "obligation" to answer without rancor or oversharing. Criticism did not bother her as long as it was done "constructively."[3] She was no pushover, however, and drew lines in the sand when she needed to. When one reader asked why her four sons couldn't "grow up like other American boys," Eleanor replied, "because you, and people like you, will not allow them to." When another reader asked about the details of F.D.R.'s marriage proposal, she replied in print, "That is a question I do not think I have any obligation to answer."[4]

Intersecting with the subjects of youth and popular culture were questions involving education, then a topic of concern due to over-crowded schools, anxieties over racial integration, and, after the successful launch of *Sputnik* in 1957, fears that the United States' educational system was inferior to that of the Soviet Union. Then, as now, the high cost of a college education, the quality of public education, and the pros and cons of private education troubled some readers. Others wanted Eleanor's advice on the best course of study for careers in politics while at least one reader wanted to know if she thought dropping out of high school to help financially needy parents was the right thing to do. (She did not.)[5]

Eleanor incorporated these issues and concerns into a broader vi-sion for American public education, one that recognized its importance both for individual development and the preservation of democracy. Local schools, she believed, should provide education while modeling a way of life and thought that demonstrated democracy in action. Public schools should also be community centers, where adults could come for education, cultural events, and other forms of intellectual renewal. At the same time, she never downplayed the value of experience be-cause she believed that "all of life is a constant education."[6]

Eleanor's views on youth, popular culture, and education re-flected her understanding that the best way to manage change was to adapt to it without losing sight of fundamental principles. In her case, her overarching concern was the creation of a well-educated citizenry capable of self-government. With technology threatening to outstrip our ability to control it, when both conspiracy theories and teenage angst can be spread across social media platforms in seconds, and when the benefits of education are simultaneously extolled and re-viled, her insight that "democracy and ignorance do not go together" is both a warning and a call to action.[7]

I am a senior in high school. I have always heard that you are the smartest woman in the world. Since this is true, which I'm positive it is, what general advice would you give a boy 17 about life?

I am afraid I am very far from being "the smartest woman in the world," and I am not fond of giving general advice to anyone. I am sure that all one can say has been said so many times to a boy of seventeen by his teachers, his parents and his pastor. I will not tell you all the obvious things—that it is better to be honest and kind than to be dishonest and selfish—but I will tell you that if you face life with a spirit of adventure and with courage you will get more out of it than if you are timid and unimaginative. [DECEMBER 1952]

Do you think a girl of seventeen is too young to go to dances?

No. I should think a girl of seventeen quite old enough to go to dances for young people of her own age. [JULY 1942]

How can I convince my mother that twelve years old is not too young to have dates?

I doubt very much if you can. I have a feeling that only a very unwise mother would consider that a girl of twelve should have dates. You are still a child and should have a good time as a child and stop thinking or wishing that you could grow up before your time. You will have a much better time in the future if you do not try to grow up too quickly. [FEBRUARY 1945]

At what age do you think a girl should be allowed to have dates with boys her own age?

I think children should naturally play with other children their own age of both sexes; and as they grow older, naturally, most of them will go skating or dancing or to the movies together. I think it is better if they can be kept in groups as long as possible, and I would hope that there would not be too much going off as individual couples before they were eighteen. [APRIL 1945]

I will soon be seventeen years old and my parents won't let me have dates. They always want me to go along with them. It seems as if they don't trust their own child. When I go without them, they want me to take my kid sister along. How can I get them to understand it is my life, and I want to have some fun?

Your parents probably enjoy your company and want you with them and do not realize that you have reached an age where you want a life of your own to some extent. I doubt very much if they do not trust you. They are trying to safeguard you from being talked about unkindly and they know that if they are with you, or if your younger sister is on hand, no one can say that you did something which you did not do.

At seventeen, however, it is understandable that you should want to have your own dates, and I think probably the best thing is for you to have a talk with your parents, explain the situation to them and learn from them what are the rules they want you to observe and then go ahead and have fun. [NOVEMBER 1947]

One of my girl friends wanted to meet the boy I go with, or did go with, and so I got her a date with a friend of his. Now she is going with my boy friend and I am left holding the bag. How can I win him back?

If I were you I would not try to win him back. If he can be taken away so easily, I do not think his affection is very deep. I would be inclined to find someone else whom I liked. Perhaps you will find that a new boy is really more attractive than the old one, and I should hope he might have a stronger character. [OCTOBER 1948]

My best friend, who is an attractive blonde, is losing all interest in life because of a certain fellow. It has been a year since they broke up. He made varsity football and doesn't seem to want to bother with her any more. How can I help her overcome her feeling for him, or advise her how to get him back again?

I think you had better be a little careful about interfering, even with your best friend. She would probably resent it, and in all probability time is what is needed to solve her problem. [NOVEMBER 1948]

I am a college girl and belong to a well-to-do family, but I am extremely unattractive. I have never had suitors and realize my chances are very slim. With this in view, what attitude should I adopt toward life?

For heaven's sake, my dear child, do not make up your mind because you are in college and haven't had any suitors that you are unattractive. Looks alone do not make one attractive. I do not know you, so I do not know just how to answer your question, but remember that one can do a great deal to improve one's personal appearance. The most important thing is what comes from the inside out. If you cultivate your mind and your spirit, you can have charm, which is far more important than looks. You may not have suitors today, but do not try too hard to have them. If you become an interesting and charming person, that will appeal to people and draw them to you when you are out of college and have a chance to make your place in the world. [JANUARY 1949]

Please give me some advice in regard to necking. I will be twenty-five in two months. I am an only child, live with my parents, am considered nice-looking, and rather shy. I have been a stenographer for three years and I am a church member. I have only dated five boys several times and each date ended in a necking bout. Is necking something that everyone does and no one admits? Do girls who refuse to neck ever get married?

My dear young lady, I think you are not very grown up in spite of your twenty-five years. I would advise you to have a few more dates and perhaps you will find among your friends boys who do not insist on necking. Probably most girls today have had some necking experiences, but I do not think that really has anything to do with whether you get married or not. [APRIL 1949]

My daughter is young and pretty and talented, but she hasn't any beaux. Friends of ours with only daughters seem to have the same difficulty. I'm afraid of meddling and making matters worse. But I'd like her to have a more satisfactory social life. What can I do?

I should think the simple thing would be to make it possible for your daughter to bring her friends to the house in a simple and easy way, never trying to do too much for them but making the young people feel welcome. If girls come, eventually boys will come too, and if your daughter does work in some organization like a church organization or the Y she is sure, sooner or later, to meet and make friends with young men as well as with other girls. [JULY 1949]

How old were you when you had your first date with a boy?

When I was young, my dear, girls did not have dates with boys; and I have absolutely no recollection of any occasions of this kind until I came out in society at the age of eighteen and gradually got to know a great many young men and women. [MARCH 1958]

I am a high-school senior of 17. I would like your honest opinion: How old should one be before she learns all the facts of life?

I am afraid one is very old before one learns all the facts of life. In fact, perhaps one comes to one's death with a humbler feeling than one had at the beginning, because the riddle of life is a difficult one to understand.

If what you mean by your question is just how old you should be before you know certain simple facts about sex, I should say that that depended entirely upon your own development. The earlier you come to look upon these facts as commonplace knowledge, the better. Everyone must acquire a certain maturity to handle these facts wisely, and nothing more. [APRIL 1948]

We are coming to you for advice because we are ashamed to go to our pastor or anyone else we know. We found out recently through a note which we discovered in our seventeen-year-old son's pocket that he and his seventeen-year-old girl friend have had illicit relations with each other for more than two years. When confronted with the evidence they defiantly admitted everything. Our son wants permission to marry this girl as he says that he loves her. Her parents do not know about them. Should we tell them and have them help us decide what should be done? We truthfully told our boy the things which he should know through the years so he did not fall into temptation and yield through ignorance. *He is conscience-stricken about the whole affair but the girl seems to be utterly devoid of a conscience.*

I think your son and the girl should go to her parents. It is their story, not yours, that has to be told. Then you and her parents could talk the situation over. It would seem to me that if you are able to do so, you would want your son to finish his education so as to be as well prepared as possible to take care of the girl he marries. Her parents, I should think, would feel that they wanted her to finish her education so that she would be well prepared to be a good wife.

In addition, two or three years may make a very great difference in both of them and the fact that they had to wait to marry until they were able to earn a living would probably mean a happier future for them and give them time to mature and realize that marriage is not just a question of physical attraction but a life companionship into which many other things have to enter if their lives are to be useful and happy together. [AUGUST 1948]

I have two young sons just entering adolescence. My husband thinks I should explain the facts of sexual maturity to them, and I think he should. We'd be interested to know how you and your husband handled this problem.

I think in the case of boys it is usually far better if their father is able to explain such things as they need to know and at the times when they need to know them. It is so important to choose the right time, not to do it too early and not to leave it till too late.

My husband was extremely shy about discussing any of these questions with our boys. I always answered any question that was asked by any of my children as truthfully as possible and told them what I thought they were able to understand, and I never told them anything which was not true. I think probably some of the masters in school were more helpful even than their father with our boys, though he did agree that he would tell them what he felt was essential. I always had an idea that he told them comparatively little! [DECEMBER 1950]

Do you think the young people of today are worse than they were ten or twenty years ago?

Certainly not. I have lived more than sixty years and I have heard young people condemned many times. I think nearly every generation is better than the last, and I certainly admire the present one. [FEBRUARY 1946]

Don't you think the sex crazied younger generation is a greater threat to civilization than the most powerful atomic bomb?

I am afraid I don't come in contact with a younger generation which is "sex crazied." I find that the vast majority of our younger generation are fine boys and girls. They are young, of course, and make mistakes (so do we all), but I love and admire them; and I must say that I think I would compare them with the good that I hope can come out of the peacetime development of atomic power but certainly not with its destructive power. [APRIL 1957]

You always defend the younger generation and say they seem so stable and fine; but if this is true, how do you explain all the wild things they do and the crimes they are committing today?

Wild things have been done by young people from time immemorial. Crimes, or the increase in them, are due to the society we develop. We have a greater population today and modern inventions make the committing of crimes by youngsters easier. They are simply using tools which were not available years ago, but in proportion to the past I think we have as great a percentage of good and fine and stable young people as ever. [SEPTEMBER 1957]

My husband wants our son to play football, and I don't. Do you think that "bodily-contact sports," as he calls them, are necessary to the development of a boy's character?

I do not know that "bodily-contact sports" are necessary to the development of a boy's character, but I do know if a boy wants to play football, and for any reason you keep him from it, you will probably find that his character—or his temper, at least—will not improve. He will probably align himself with his father and you will be left on the outside, so I advise you not to be too vocal about your feelings. [JANUARY 1942]

My twelve-year-old son is forever after his father to buy him a rifle. The whole idea terrifies me. Don't you think he's too young? What did you do when your boys asked to have guns?

I think when a boy wants a gun it is not enough just to buy it for him. The father must teach his son how to use it and teach him the proper safeguards that must always be observed. If the boy does not observe them he should forfeit the gun for a certain length of time. Twelve years does not seem too young to be taught, and he may be a good shot. Many boys are at that age. The important thing isn't whether he has the gun but whether he has been taught to use it with care and discretion. [MARCH 1951]

Do you think it is correct for a girl of fifteen to wear lipstick and powder?

Personally, I would put it off as long as I could. I don't suppose it can be put off after eighteen; but if it could be put off that long, I should do so because the girl's skin will be better if too much powder is not used on it while she is still young. [NOVEMBER 1945]

Do you think sixteen-year-old boys should be allowed to drive cars?

It depends on the sixteen-year-old's sense of responsibility. They should certainly be allowed to drive cars with older people accompanying them, because that is the way to learn how to drive. Whether they should be allowed to go into crowded thoroughfares, alone, is a question of the ability and sense of responsibility of the individual sixteen-year-old boy. [MAY 1942]

I am a fifteen-year-old girl in senior high. I would like your straight opinion on teen-age girls' personalities today. I mean how a girl's personality should be.

It is a little difficult to tell you what your personality should be when you are still in your teens. In the first place, everybody in the world is different, and if you are wise you will not try to copy someone else, but you will try to develop what you have within you, to the best of your ability. The most attractive personality is always the most natural one, and the one which is least affected and the least bothered by self-consciousness.

A girl in her teens cannot have a great deal of personality because she hasn't lived long enough, but she can be gay, thoughtful of others and interested in life. That will give her a good foundation on which to build a richer personality as she grows older. [JUNE 1945]

I am seventeen, a senior in high school, and have spent every one of my teen-age years in misery because of self-consciousness. I cannot look a person in the eye even to say "Hello" without getting a funny expression on my face, and to give an oral report in school is almost torture. Whenever anyone as much as glances at me, I feel as though he is criticizing me. This bashfulness not only causes me great unhappiness, but affects my marks. The one and only thing I am looking forward to in life is marrying and having a large family. I really love kids more than any other thing in this world. And I realize my dream will remain a dream if I do not snap out of this present condition. Please, Mrs. Roosevelt, is there any way I can do this?

Surely. If you will just stop thinking about yourself and begin to think about other people, you can make them and yourself happier. You can help them if you can find something to do for them. If you like children, get some fun out of being with them and do not think about whether people are watching you or not. Believe me, when you think people are criticizing you, they probably haven't even given you a thought. It is remarkable how unconscious most people are about other people. If you can just remember that, in starting out to do the kind of things that any human being does who lets himself be natural, you will soon make friends. [MARCH 1947]

My teen-age daughter, who is five feet ten, is getting a complex about her height. Could you give us some practical advice—anything you wish someone had told you about being tall when you were young?

Tell her to hold herself straight and not to allow herself to slump and bend over. It is difficult to be tall for your age when you are young, but while there are obvious disadvantages, you can also see over other people's heads in a crowd! If you hold yourself well, people will not think so much about your being tall, and the best thing to do is just to forget about your height and then others will forget about it too. [SEPTEMBER 1956]

Don't you think a girl of twenty-one should be able to decide a few things for herself, without having her parents do it for her?

I certainly do think a girl of twenty-one should be able to decide anything for herself. At twenty-one many girls are married and directing their own households; but I think if a girl wants to decide for herself, she must be quite sure she has prepared herself to make wise decisions. She must be a disciplined person, and she cannot make hasty decisions, and she must seek advice where she is not experienced and needs it. [NOVEMBER 1941]

I have been holding my own in the business world for almost five years, but my mother still does not think it suitable for me to have my own apartment. Do you think I should stay at home obediently?

It depends entirely, I think, on the kind of relationship you want in your home. If you want to carry on a very close family life, it is certainly better for you to live at home. However, if you find that as you have grown older and more independent, it creates friction to live with the family, perhaps it would be better for you to have your own apartment. You might find you could really have a pleasanter and happier relationship with your family by actually living apart. I think every woman, if she does not marry, craves a home of her own, and perhaps you could explain that to your mother. [MARCH 1946]

We have to hide some of the magazines from our adolescent children because of the references to liquor. What can we do about it?

I cannot imagine why you should hide magazines from your adolescent children because they have references to liquor. Do you think your children can live in this world and not know that liquor exists, or that the use of it is condemned when it is used to excess, but that it is a commodity on the market? I am afraid our adolescent children are not dependent for their information on the magazines which they find in their own homes, and the effort to hide them will be of little use. I should be inclined to tell them whatever you want them to know. They have to live in this world, so you have to trust them in the end. [FEBRUARY 1947]

Don't you think parents have an obligation to exercise some supervision over their children's choice of companions? If you had a seventeen-year-old daughter who was spending most of her time with rude, uncouth boys and girls, wouldn't you use every means at your command to separate her from them?

If your daughter is choosing her friends from among youngsters of this sort, I'm afraid you haven't given her enough of your time and have not encouraged her to bring her friends home. A child whose friends are welcome in her home soon learns to distinguish between the desirable and undesirable, since differences show up clearly in this atmosphere. To use strong-arm tactics at this point will only antagonize a seventeen-year-old. Your best plan is to think of activities that will interest her and attract well-behaved schoolmates. [JUNE 1962]

Did you have to cope with the awkward age in your daughter? If so, how did you do it and keep the family fur from flying? I have a daughter, sixteen, who wants to wear her dresses too tight and too old, and wrong shades of make-up. She also has a strange taste in friends and keeps too late hours. How can I avoid argument, yet instill in her some ideas of good behavior and good taste?

Of course every youngster, boy or girl, goes through an awkward stage, and family fur will fly, and you cannot avoid arguments. I can remember very well periods when my children felt very bitterly toward me, but we became firm friends again as they grew older and realized there was sense in what I made them do and in what I said. The important thing is to love them and they soon know you are not just trying to be disagreeable—which they often think! [OCTOBER 1946]

Our eighteen-year-old son has a unique chance to travel around the world with relatives and live in various countries for the next two years. This will mean entering college two years later than he should, if at all, and his father and I don't know what to decide. An opinion from you would help us a lot.

How about asking your eighteen-year-old son what he would like to do? Two years of travel is a good preparation for life in the present-day world. I myself would not like to consider this a substitute for college, but something which would make his college years more worthwhile. It is true that he will not have the companionship of his own age group, but if he is convinced that the travel will help him, he will certainly use it to good advantage. I feel strongly that the final decision should rest with him. At eighteen you are old enough to know what you want to do and where you want to go. [NOVEMBER 1958]

I guess you'll be rather surprised to hear from a boy, but I've got a problem. I am nineteen years old. My mother considers me a child and my father thinks I am as much of a man as he is. Isn't that a mess? I look at it this way. The Army thought I was old enough to go to war. Why am I a child at home? I went with a girl before I went overseas, and now I am starting out in a new and good job. I love her very much, and we would like to get married in a few months, but it would cause a complete eruption in my home. All I need is some way to make mother see the light and understand what I want to do.

Nineteen is rather young to get married, though I realize that having been in the war and overseas, you are probably mature for your years. That may not, however, be the case for the girl, and possibly your mother is not so much disturbed because she thinks you are a child, as because she feels that both of you, in the course of the next few years or so, may change, as so often happens, and then you might find you have made a mistake and were not as compatible as one should be in a life partnership. I think you have every right to demand that you be treated as a man at home, and be given freedom in every possible way; but if your mother asks you to wait a year, even though you are both anxious to get married and you have a good job, remember there are many years ahead of you. A man who marries, at twenty-one, a girl who is perhaps a year or two younger than himself still has a long period to enjoy the happiness which he has waited for. Of course I do not know what the special circumstances may be, and I am only giving you advice in a very general way, because in almost every case there are special reasons which might well change the point of view which a stranger like myself holds. [DECEMBER 1946]

Although I am 19, I look only about 16. Maybe this is why my parents have always treated me like such a baby. I was never allowed to go out with boys until I was a senior in high school. I was married shortly after I graduated and am going to have a child soon. We have been married almost a year and have never had a real fight. I am happier than I have ever been. My problem is that my parents never have approved our marriage and seem to resent my husband. How can I help to change this?

I do not like to give advice in such intimate family matters as these, where the feelings of the individuals involved enter into the solution.

In a general way, however, I should say that it might be that your parents found it hard to adjust to having a child, whom they had always regarded as a baby, actually living a life of her own and belonging primarily to her husband. If that is the cause, it will take time and patience both on your part and on your husband's part, and an effort on the part of your parents, to realize that all people grow up and that parents often have to develop interests of their own when their children leave them. [AUGUST 1947]

A group of us are trying to build up interest in national politics by campaigning for our high-school student council and class officers. I have discussed this with the principal and American history teacher, and they are in favor of it. Can you give any suggestions on how to get and keep the students' interest? The principal has agreed to let us have assemblies and campus campaigning.

If there is any way in which the problems which you face in your school can be tied up with the questions that are being discussed in your community, state, and nation, then I think you will find that in a very painless way you can lead the members of the student body to think about their government. For instance, if you have any racial questions that you face, you can tie them up with the racial questions which we face in the nation. Discrimination can exist in school, and it can be wiped out in school in just the same way that it should be wiped out in the nation. I think if you can get some local speaker to explain to you special subjects that touch your lives, that may help to broaden your interests. For instance, every boy and girl today is touched by the draft, and an understanding of the reasons for military preparation and the hope of peace in the future generation and disarmament among nations could be quite easy to tie up with your school interests. [OCTOBER 1948]

How old do you think a child should be before he gets a dog of his own?

A child should not have a dog of his own until he or she is able to take care of it, dependable enough to attend to the dog's wants daily without being told and has enough common sense not to hurt the dog or be unkind to it out of thoughtlessness. [FEBRUARY 1953]

If you were a boy twelve years old and your parents wouldn't let you have a dog, what would you do?

I think I would do my best to persuade my parents that I was a responsible person who would take care of a dog if I were allowed to have one. Most parents object to a dog because they think their children will not take full responsibility, will forget to feed it and exercise it and the animal will become more of a burden on the grownups than on the boy. If you can persuade your parents that you can be completely trusted to care for a dog and will avoid allowing the dog to become a nuisance to them, I think they will be more inclined to let you have one. [AUGUST 1945]

My dog died. I am so upset about this that I don't hear my mother when she talks to me and I can't do my homework. Can you tell me what to do?

You must be very young, and this is probably your first real sorrow. Time will help you to bear it, and I am sorry that the companionship with your dog had to come to an end, but you must remember that dogs' lives are always shorter than the lives of human beings. We ought to make their lives as happy as possible and be grateful for every moment of love and happiness that they give us, but at best it should not be tragic when the parting comes if we have done our part in giving them a happy time while they are on earth with us. [MAY 1953]

I have heard that you are one of the advisory editors of a comic magazine. Do you think comic books suitable reading for children?

I think some comic books are suitable reading for children. They should, however, be carefully chosen. I wrote in my column on April 25, 1941, about *True Comics*, edited by David Marke, published by Parents Institute. I later refused to be chairman or honorary chairman for another publisher. [DECEMBER 1942]

Everybody makes such a terrible fuss about "rock 'n' roll." Wasn't there just as big a fuss over things like the Charleston? Frankly, do you think rock 'n' roll is any more shocking than the black bottom was in the twenties?

I know I am behind the times but I've never seen rock and roll, and I am sorry to say that I don't know what the black bottom was. However, the fad will probably pass just as many of the other excitements which have seized our youth at various times are now forgotten. I agree with you that we needn't take it too seriously. [DECEMBER 1956]

My wife and I had a big fight about the Kinsey report. She feels a book like this puts unhealthy thoughts in people's minds. I think it will probably do more good than harm. What is your opinion?

I think I feel as your wife does. This report is for mature people who want to read it because they can use the knowledge. I do not think it should be in the hands of people who consider it light and entertaining. [FEBRUARY 1951]

What do you think of the increasing tendency of today's novelists to use so many "four-letter words" not spoken in polite society?

I did not know there were any words left that were not spoken in polite society. [OCTOBER 1941]

What do you think is the reason that profanity is not only accepted in "polite society," but actually seems to be approved? How can I teach my children not to use such expressions when they hear them from people they admire?

I think the use of certain expressions is not regarded as profanity by a good many young people. Even some older people have come to use these expressions as a method of emphasizing their remarks. They would use a slang phrase or a descriptive word in much the same way, and I do not think, as a rule, it is done with any idea of actually being profane. If you do not want your children to use any expression, it is best to explain your reasons, and they will often follow your example. I think what troubles you is just a temporary and passing thing and probably will cease to be the fashion in a few years' time. [DECEMBER 1944]

Are you in favor of legalized lotteries?

I do not know a great deal about the subject, but on the whole I think I am against legalizing gambling as you do in a lottery. [MARCH 1945]

Do you ever watch television? What is your favorite program?

I watch television only when I want to see certain special programs. And if I possibly can, I watch when the President of the United States appears; or when any other public official speaks on a subject on which I think citizens should be informed. I have no favorite program, since I have no time to listen or watch just for pleasure. [AUGUST 1959]

Why aren't you on a regular radio or TV program any more? We used to listen to all your programs, and now we can never find any.

I am glad to know that you listened to my programs and would still like to have me on TV and radio. I would like to go back if possible but I did so much traveling in the last year it was not possible for me to give the necessary time. I am not sure how much time I will have in the coming year, nor am I sure any advertiser will feel like sponsoring a program on which I appear. There are people who dislike me wholeheartedly as well as people who like me, and for a sponsored program perhaps a noncontroversial figure is best. [APRIL 1953]

What did you hope to accomplish by appearing on a TV commercial that you could not accomplish some other way?

I am getting older and may not be able to travel as much as I have in the past. I like to keep in touch with people, and one reaches large numbers by radio and TV. My agent had found that most people considered me too controversial to advertise anything profitably, and so when an offer to do a commercial came, I felt that unless I did it, we would never know whether I had any commercial value on the air. I do not yet know whether it was a wise or an unwise thing to do, but I thought it worth a trial. [JULY 1959]

Would you like to see our system of commercially sponsored television replaced either by a pay-TV system or by the British system of separating advertisers from program control?

I think there is much to be said for the British system. I have never been quite convinced of the real value of paid TV. If one could get certain types of program that were not interrupted by commercials, it would be a great advantage. [MAY 1961]

Don't you think the radio's singing commercials are a reflection on the intelligence of the American people?

No, I do not think they are a reflection on the intelligence of the American public but I think perhaps they are an indication that the average advertiser thinks that the American buying public is attracted to his wares by somewhat juvenile methods. The advertiser may be right, and who am I to criticize, for I rarely buy anything which I hear advertised over the radio. [JULY 1946]

Does the money you get from those hearing aid advertisements* go to charity? If not, I just cannot understand your lowering yourself in that way?

I can't see that it lowers one in any way to let people know through an advertisement that a hearing aid or anything else has been help-

---

*   In the 1950s, Eleanor Roosevelt appeared in newspaper ads endorsing different brands of hearing aids. See https://1gm8d73foqeh1436341icth6-wpengine.netdna-ssl.com/wp-content/uploads/2012/08/eleanor-roosevelt-hearing-aid-ad.jpg for an example.

ful. In the matter you mention it happens that the only financial transaction was a gift to the Wiltwyck School, which is one of the charities I am most interested in. [AUGUST 1957]

Except in the matter of anesthetics, do you think the world any better place than it was when you were young?

Yes, I do think the world is a better place than it was when I was young. There are more people in it who are conscious of the inequalities and injustices of our social setup and who are making an effort to bring these questions out in the open so that the public may become conscious of them and some better solutions be found. Education reaches more people, and there are more enjoyments possible in consequence. Besides anesthetics, many other discoveries and inventions make life easier and pleasanter for human beings. [JUNE 1941]

Ladies Home Journal co-editor Bruce Gould originally envisioned "If You Ask Me" as a vehicle to combat "the rumors, innuendoes and backstairs gossip about the inhabitants of the White House," as well as a way for Eleanor Roosevelt to answer "other queries about which the public, rightly or wrongly, thinks it has a right to know." Of all the types of questions readers submitted, the largest number fall into the "curiosity" or "voyeurism" category. The following questions are a representative sample.[8]

Will you please tell me how you manage to answer, in such a friendly, courteous and considerate manner, the rude and impertinent questions asked you? Aren't you sometimes tempted to refuse to continue this column?

I never think of questions as being rude and impertinent. I have accepted the assignment of answering a page of questions once every month, and anyone has a right to ask whatever he feels inclined to ask. It is perfectly natural that there should be people who like neither me nor my ideas nor my husband and what he stands for in public life, and if they choose to ask questions I have an obligation to answer them.

I would not do this page unless I thought it was worth doing—not just because I am paid for it, but because I hope there is some actual value in the flow of ideas which is bound to come from honest questions and honest answers—so I am never tempted to discontinue the page, nor have I ever refused to answer a question. [MAY 1943]

Do you do all your own writing, or do you sometimes use a ghost?

I have never used a ghost. I have worked with other people and have had a great deal of help, which I am always anxious to acknowledge, both in organizing my material and presenting it better; but the material has always been mine. [FEBRUARY 1960]

Do you have a special way of making yourself inconspicuous when you don't want people to recognize you in public places?

No. I only move very quickly. I find if I never look at anyone and move fast I am frequently not recognized. [JANUARY 1953]

I know you never wanted to be famous, but I get the feeling that celebrities can't help developing a taste for fame and would feel lost and lonely without it. Am I at all right about this in your case?

I really don't know, because I never thought about it. I have never felt famous. I have done whatever was offered me to do whenever I could, but if opportunities did not come I am quite sure I should not feel either lost or lonely. I would go about my own business, narrowing down to a more intimate, personal circle and in many ways, I imagine, being happier for this opportunity of deepening contacts rather than spreading them so thin. [MAY 1954]

How have you been able to develop such a sense of fairness, good will, kindness, tolerance and serenity?

You are very kind to attribute so many good qualities to me. I am afraid that with the amount of publicity and controversy which have surrounded me and my family for a great many years, I would either have become an embittered old lady or a nervous wreck if I had not been able to decide on what I thought was right and become indifferent to what other people thought, unless they were people whose opinion I respected and valued. [OCTOBER 1943]

Have you noticed that there are fewer unkind remarks about you in the press in recent years? Do you think there is any special reason for this?

Perhaps it is just because I am growing old and people know they will not have to put up with me for many more years, so they are more kindly disposed when I do or say things with which they disagree. [DECEMBER 1957]

How do you explain the fact that you've grown much better-looking as you've grown older?

I thank you for the compliment. It simply means that as you grow older, people don't expect you to be as good-looking as they expect a young person to be, so they are kinder in their judgments. [AUGUST 1958]

Bette Davis' pet economy is using the same bobby pins several years. What is yours?

Saving string. [JULY 1941]

Do you ever give to beggars on the street? If so, how do you justify it?

Yes, I do occasionally give to beggars on the street. When I lived in my own home I made it a point to take people home to feed them rather than to give them money, and then to help them in any way possible to get a job if that was what they needed. Now that is impossible. However, when I see someone who looks fairly desperate, I would rather give money, on the chance of sometimes giving unwisely, than to withhold it from some one person who might need a helping hand and who deserves it. [NOVEMBER 1942]

In a magazine article I read that you have trained yourself so that you can take short naps when you have a little free time during the day. I have heard of other people being able to do this. Are there any words of instruction or advice that you could give to help another person develop this ability?

I would only suggest that you be so tired that you cannot keep your eyes open. If you are as weary as that and have learned to relax instead of becoming keyed up and tense, you will find that your eyes will close and you will be asleep for a few minutes until some unexpected sound awakens you. It may be for one or three or five minutes, but the principle requirement is that you be very weary, and still able to relax. Don't do it in an automobile, however, unless you pull off the road first! [OCTOBER 1948]

What is your greatest fear?

My greatest fear has always been that I would be afraid—afraid physically or mentally or morally—and allow myself to be influenced by fear instead of by my honest convictions. [AUGUST 1942]

Whom do you fear most in the world today?

I do not think I fear anyone. [AUGUST 1951]

What do you do for fun?

I go to the country, see my friends, read, go to the theater and to concerts. [JUNE 1944]

What did the President say to you when he proposed?

That is a question that I do not think I have any obligation to answer. There are some things in life which one should be allowed to keep to oneself. [JULY 1944]

Have you ever thought of marrying again?

No. [APRIL 1951]

Do you number among your friends any who could be considered as "poor people" financially?

Many! [JUNE 1957]

Although the Roosevelts and their children had owned dogs before and during their time in the White House, none captured
the public's imagination like Fala, the Scottish terrier given to
F.D.R. by his cousin Margaret "Daisy" Suckley in 1940. Fala fol-
lowed F.D.R. everywhere and quickly became as much a part of
his public image as his jaunty smile and cigarette holder. Thanks
to extensive media coverage, he also became the best-known dog
in America, especially after F.D.R. used him in a 1944 campaign
speech to refute a Republican charge of presidential extrava-
gance: "Fala is Scottish," the president said, "and being a Scottie,
as soon as he learned that the Republican fiction writers in Congress and out had concocted a story that I had left him behind
on the Aleutian Islands (where F.D.R. had traveled earlier that
year) and had sent a destroyer back to find him—at a cost to the
taxpayers of two or three or eight or twenty million dollars—his
Scotch soul was furious. He has not been the same dog since." [9]

*Being Scottie lovers, my family and I have often wondered about Presi-
dent Roosevelt's little dog Fala. What age did he live to be? Is he
perhaps buried at Hyde Park? Does he have any descendants? And do
you have any Scotties now?*

Fala lived to be thirteen years old. He is buried in the rose garden
at Hyde Park, near the sundial. Next to him is the first dog my
daughter owned, which was a great favorite of my husband's—a

police dog named Chief. Each has a little oval stone with his name on it. Fala has descendants, though I don't happen to own any of them. I have a little Scottie, given me by some sweet children in Ohio, whose dog had a litter of puppies at the time Fala died. His name is Duffy and he lives at Hyde Park. [SEPTEMBER 1961]

What do you consider a successful life for a man? For a woman?

A successful life for a man or for a woman seems to me to lie in the knowledge that one has developed to the limit the capacities with which one was endowed; that one has contributed something constructive to family and friends and to a home community; that one has brought happiness wherever it was possible; that one has earned one's way in the world, has kept some friends and need not be ashamed to face oneself honestly. [NOVEMBER 1941]

What do you think are the three most important requisites for happiness?

A feeling that you have been honest with yourself and with those around you; a feeling that you have done the best you could both in your personal life and in your work; and the ability to love others. [OCTOBER 1946]

Do you have a philosophy of life you could put into a few words?

I have never given very deep thought to a philosophy of life, though I have a few ideas that I think are useful to me. One is that you do whatever comes your way to do as well as you can, and another is that you think as little as possible about yourself and as much as possible about other people and about things that are interesting. The third is that you get more joy out of giving joy to others and should put a good deal of thought into the happiness that you are able to give. [SEPTEMBER 1957]

Your philosophy and, indeed, your life seem to be dedicated to doing things for others. Most Americans have felt it was the things individuals or groups or nations did for themselves that they valued most highly. Don't you think it's possible to rob persons and peoples of these accomplishments by doing too much for them? Do you, as an individual, welcome or resist the efforts of others to do things for you?

I think that people, both as individuals and as nations, need help. If the help is given in the proper spirit and in the proper way, it will not rob them of a sense of their own accomplishment. No amount of outside help can really achieve the full result of what people want for themselves; but unless they get some help, they may never be able to accomplish some of the things they want most. I am most grateful for the innumerable things people do for me, and I could not possibly live my life unless I accepted a great deal of help from others. I do have to love the people, however, and feel that what they do is done willingly and affectionately. Otherwise, I might feel that the help had ulterior motives or was grudgingly given. [AUGUST 1960]

Do you think a girl with a fairly well-paying job, whose parents need help, should stop going to school? I am in my second year of high school.

Not unless it is absolutely necessary; because while the girl might give her parents temporary help as long as the job lasts, she would cut off her chance of earning more money in the future, and of preparing herself not only for a better-paying job but for more enjoyment along cultural lines which would be made possible by more education. [NOVEMBER 1942]

I would like to know your opinion of aptitude tests. I am unhappy in my work as a stenographer, and although I have had training and four years' experience in this kind of work, I have not been a success. Since I am not working now, it would be a good time to look into the possibilities of some other type of work.

If I were in your position, I certainly should take aptitude tests, and if I had any interests I had never tried to develop, I should try to develop them to see if I enjoyed working along some particular new line. [JULY 1947]

Do you think it unpatriotic for boys and girls to attend college in these times if they are financially able to do so?

I think it deplorable to consider attending college simply from the point of view of whether you are financially able to do so or not. I have always felt that in a democracy, somehow, we should arrange so that all young people consider the opportunity for higher education, not from the point of view of finances, but from the point of view of what they desire to do in life and their ability to do it. It certainly has nothing to do with patriotism either, since, if the Government needs you, whether you are attending college or not, you will be called by the Government; but the Government realizes that young people who really intend to do work which will fit them to be more useful in the world are doing a valuable service either by going to college or, if that is not the type of work they intend to do, by taking courses which will make them skilled workers. [OCTOBER 1942]

I am seventeen years old and have just finished high school. My mother insists that I go on to college, but I would rather take a job on the newspaper at home. Mother says I will always regret missing college, but it seems to me the women I admire most in public life never went to college. Don't you think the world is better training for a newspaper-woman than the classroom?

I am afraid I do not agree with you. There are certain kinds of knowledge acquired in the classroom—history, grammar, a knowledge of literature—which, if you want to be a really good newspaperwoman, will be invaluable to your career.

My husband always complained bitterly that even some of the best newspapermen lacked sufficient knowledge of certain countries when he visited them and that he was constantly briefing them on trips to give them more background which would make their stories more interesting and understandable.

I know it is hard, when you want to take a job, to stick to the kind of work college means when you are not going to college just to enjoy yourself. But if you are serious in making newspaper work your career, you had better get as good a background and training as you possibly can. [SEPTEMBER 1950]

Our teen-age daughter is very much interested in politics as a career. She and we have tried to discover what kind of education is the best preparation for such a career, but no one seems very sure. Do you think a law degree is necessary; and if not, what college course would you recommend?

I don't believe politics is a career you can prepare for. In our country, I think, it is much better to have an occupation you enjoy and are successful in. Then, if you have the urge to run for elective office or accept an appointive office, you can do so and feel free, because you can always return to your original occupation with pleasure and profit. In this way, no one can intimidate you by saying that if you do this or that, you will not be re-elected or reappointed. You will be free, without any consideration or expediency, to do what is right; and this makes for a better public servant. A good all-around general education, with some specialization in history and government and economics, is the best preparation. But this background would also be good preparation for many other careers. [APRIL 1961]

The cost of education is rising so rapidly that fewer and fewer parents will be able to send their children to college without absolutely strapping themselves. Have you any opinion about government subsidy for qualified students?

It seems to me imperative that we accept the fact that we can no longer afford to waste our human material the way we are doing. Too many young people do not prepare for college, because they are afraid they will not have an opportunity to go. Others prepare, and then there is no money to send them to college. I think we are a rich enough country to provide all children capable of it with higher education. Going to college should depend on ability and not on finances. The cost should be borne by all taxpayers as it is for public elementary and high schools. [FEBRUARY 1960]

Do you think that, after the war, discipline rather than democratic self-expression should be emphasized in the education of young people?

I have always thought that discipline was an indispensable part of education, but I think it is quite possible, also to have democratic self-expression. Democratic self-expression does not mean that a child has to be thoughtless of those around him, or through self-indulgence make life for everyone else miserable. It does mean that within the limits of a proper discipline, freedom should be allowed to every individual for personal development. [MAY 1943]

In some public schools they are making it compulsory for children to learn a foreign language in the early grades. How do you feel about this?

I am delighted to hear that this is being done. The earlier children learn a foreign language the easier it is. In the earlier years children learn almost everything by memory and by ear, and not by reasoning. Arithmetic, which calls for reasoning, is difficult for small children. Languages, if learned while children are young, are learned largely by ear, and not by grammar, and children get an accent better and find the language easier than if they wait until they are older. It is most important for our young people to learn languages now, since they are likely to work and be in countries all over the world. Making friends in foreign countries is easier if you know the language of the people you are with. [JANUARY 1954]

Do you think Federal aid for schools would help raise our educational standards in poor communities?

I certainly do. I have wanted to see us have Federal aid for schools for a long while because our educational opportunities are so uneven throughout the nation. [JULY 1946]

Don't you think that both education and racial discrimination could be helped by taking public education away from the states altogether and bringing it under the control of the Federal Government, so that it could be the same all over the country?

I think it would be a pity to take education away from the states. I believe in Federal aid to the states and in equalizing the opportunity for all children as quickly as it can be done, but the smaller unit is important, since it knows more about the teachers and children within the state than the National Government. The National Government may well set standards below which no state must fall. For instance, a certain number of school weeks in a year, a certain rate of pay for teachers, a certain standard of education where teachers are concerned, and so on; but to turn the entire control over to the Federal Government would, I think, not be an improvement. [OCTOBER 1947]

How do you feel about a child's being tutored at home? Were any of yours?

Many of my children were tutored at different times at home. I nearly always had someone to teach them in the summer the things I felt they had not learned enough about in the winter. My husband also was tutored at home in his early years because his father was delicate and the family spent a great deal of time at health resorts in Europe. But if you mean do I prefer tutoring at home to going to school, then I must say I feel quite strongly that a child should go to school. The companionship a child gets in school is an important part of his education. [SEPTEMBER 1958]

What do you think of sending three-year-olds to nursery school? Doesn't that seem awfully young?

No, not for nursery school. Nursery schools often take children from one and a half to two years old, and I have seen many of them profit greatly by the experience. The hours are not too long, and the child is fed and is allowed to rest during the period. I think the contact with other children and the discipline are excellent. Besides, sending children to nursery school gives our modern young mothers, who have a great deal to do, time to do their work while the youngest of their children are well cared for outside the home. [MARCH 1960]

How much do you blame "progressive education" for the poor level of students in this country?

I do not blame progressive education at all. Progressive education, properly used and understood, should have helped us and not brought about a lower standard of learning for our students. Our present low standards, I feel, are due to indifference on the part of older people and to the general attitude that education is a right rather than a privilege calling for real responsibility. [OCTOBER 1958]

I am sure all your children went to private schools, not because you are a snobbish person, which I know you are not, but because you could afford it. What would you advise a person to do who has several children in a city where the public schools are downright dreadful, but who cannot afford the luxury of a private school?

Of course, in that case, there is no alternative. The children must go to public schools, and I would advise that, as residents of the area, you join with others in working and agitating for better schools. I have always felt it was a pity that so many people sent their children to private schools, because they are then less likely to work for improved public schools. My children went to private schools because of tradition. I fought it for a time, but my mother-in-law and husband made the final decision. I think private schools have an advantage in being able to do a certain amount of experimentation that public schools have come to more slowly. But I believe that, for the good of the community, more of us should have children in public schools, so we can fight together for better schools. [MARCH 1961]

What is your opinion of the idea of teaching religion in the public schools?

I do not think that religion can properly be taught in public schools. We decided long ago to separate church and state. The public schools, being financed and run by the states, should not teach religion to children. That should be the responsibility of the home and the church primarily, though it may be possible in certain cases to work out some form of spiritual expression which is acceptable to all the children in a school. I feel, however, this should never be forced upon any of them. [DECEMBER 1948]

Don't you think that the trend toward eliminating report cards in the schools may make weaklings of our children? Competition, it seems to me, is just as much the lifeblood of the classroom as it is of the country.

I hardly think that report cards will be entirely eliminated, since parents will always want to know how children are progressing according to their teachers' observation. The elimination of exams and the constant competition in marks may be a good thing, because for some children this competition creates a great deal of anxiety. They are pretty sure to have competition in so much that they do in life that if they can learn to enjoy knowledge for its own sake it should be a very good thing. [JULY 1954]

What ten books should one read before considering oneself well educated?

I am afraid there are no ten books which will educate anyone. Education is not merely a question of reading ten books. You might get from a library a list of ten books that everyone should read, but that would not mean that because you read them you were educated. Education goes on all the days of our lives and is acquired not only in school but in actual living. [AUGUST 1948]

When one is deprived of a college education today, does it necessarily mean that he must live in the stages of mediocrity, or is it still possible for him to clash wits with college graduates? In this period of competitive practice, what attributes must be attained to climb the ladder of success?

I do not think that not having a college education you must of necessity be mediocre all your life. I know many men and women who never had a college education who have reached a fairly satisfactory educational level and are doing as good a job of holding their own as those who had the advantage of a college education. It is true that in getting your initial job at the present time it is an advantage to have a college degree and, of course, if you are going into any of the professions you must have it, besides your graduate work. However, in the fields where a college education is not essential if you educate yourself continuously I think you can compete quite well with college graduates. [AUGUST 1949]

Do you think eventually all schools and colleges in the country will be coeducational? Is this desirable?

I rather hope the trend toward making schools coeducational will never be completely universal. Among my dozens of grandchildren, grandnieces and grandnephews, and their friends, I find some with tremendous enthusiasm for the coeducational schools they attend, and others with at least equal enthusiasm for their all-men or all-girl colleges. I like the idea that young people will always have some choice, since it seems to me it is one important way of avoiding total conformity. [OCTOBER 1962]

Do you think there is much to be gained from giving children a shorter summer vacation and longer school year as some educators are now suggesting?

Yes. Our present summer vacations are so very long that most children lose a good many of their school habits. If we do this, however, it might be advisable to lengthen the Easter or the Christmas holidays and in these periods to give young people some assignment, such as outside reading, which is difficult to do when schoolwork has to be done as well. [MAY 1958]

Well-qualified, well-paid teachers capable of stimulating their students' intellect, curiosity, and creativity were key to making Eleanor Roosevelt's educational vision a reality. To that end, she consistently advocated on their behalf for better educational opportunities, higher salaries, and increased respect.[10]

What is your opinion of schools that refuse to hire teachers over 45?

Young people are often preferred, but I would feel that a proper proportion of older people was a good balance in any school. [JANUARY 1955]

If you had the time and opportunity to teach in a college for a year, what college would you prefer and what subject would you like to teach?

I would like to teach either American history or American literature. I have no preference as to the college because I have never had enough experience with any of them to know what the differences among them might be. [JUNE 1956]

We hear a great deal about raising the salaries of teachers as a way of improving the quality of our education. We also hear that the caliber of our present teachers is often not nearly so high as it should be. Yet these are the very people whose salaries we are told we should raise. I do not believe more money is going to make good teachers out of inferior ones. Do you?

Certainly not. However, in an economy where the gauge of one's importance or of one's success is the amount of money one makes, it is quite evident that if we think teaching is an important career, it must be adequately rewarded. Just raising the salaries of teachers is not going to improve the caliber of the present ones. But it will, in the long run, attract to the teaching profession better-qualified people. When we have better-qualified teachers, I hope the role of the teacher in the community automatically will become more and more dignified, more respected. A gain in teachers' status will give us better-qualified personnel. At the same time, however, we must improve the quality of the instruction in our teacher-training institutions all over the country. We have not always seen to it that the best possible preparation is given the young people who decide to devote their lives to the teaching profession. [JANUARY 1961]

Do you think teachers should be unionized, with the right to strike?

I think it right that they should be unionized, and if we pay so little attention to their interests that they are obliged to strike, it is the fault of the community and not of the teacher. I know that there has often been a feeling against the unionization of professional people; but it is increasingly obvious that such people can often not get proper attention, because they do not have bargaining power. It is evident that when the health or well-being of any section of the population is concerned, the right to strike has some limitations. There might be some qualifications necessary in the case of teachers; but I firmly believe that if you take away certain rights, you have to give greater protection in return. [MARCH 1962]

Chapter 9

WAR AND PEACE

N<small>UCLEAR WAR, NORTH KOREA</small>, the Middle East, America's role in the world, the usefulness of the United Nations, U.S. military incursions into foreign countries, negotiating (or not) with the Russians and the Chinese, maintaining peace—Eleanor Roosevelt would find much that pops up on our daily newsfeeds familiar because she lived with many of the same tensions. Unlike some of her contemporaries who took refuge in despair, isolationism, or conspiracy theories, she did not succumb to fear and suspicion. Instead she advocated engagement with the world and action to solve its problems.

The question of engagement was unavoidable when Eleanor began writing "If You Ask Me" in the spring of 1941. Then, Americans were wrestling with how to respond to conflicts in Europe and Asia. Seven months later the Japanese attack on Pearl Harbor made the issue moot.

After World War II, Americans debated the United States's role in the postwar world and the best way to build a sustainable peace in the nuclear era. Once again there were those who wanted to retreat into isolationism and those who despaired this time over the inevitability of nuclear holocaust. More ominously, others thought the United States should use nuclear weapons to solve its Cold War conflicts with communist-led nations in Europe and Asia.

Eleanor refused to believe that nuclear war was necessary or inevitable. A confirmed internationalist, she devoted much of the last seventeen years of her life to the causes of peace and international understanding because she knew that "nobody wins a modern war."[1] Through her work with the United Nations and her own international travels she understood in ways that many of her contemporaries did not that World War II had changed the world irrevocably. Newly independent countries in Africa, Asia, and the Middle East were emerging from their colonial pasts; new technologies were making transportation and communication faster; and the world's population was exploding, stressing both governments and the environment. If Americans want to prosper and remain free and secure they had to understand, accept, and live by the adage that "the world cannot be understood from a single point of view."[2]

In her view, dialogue between individuals from different cultures and between nations offered America and the world the best chance for long-term peace. She acknowledged that dialogue was a messy process; disagreement was inevitable, and unity would often prove elusive. Still the effort had to continue because "words, even when they seem to fail to communicate, are better than bombs," a pertinent reminder for a world grappling with the proliferation of nuclear weapons, terrorist attacks, and cyberwarfare.[3]

For many Americans, the war years were a period of distress and dislocation. Millions of American families had relatives in the military, while more than fifteen million civilians migrated to various parts of the country seeking work. The explosive growth of the defense industry placed severe strains on housing, education, and medical facilities, especially in areas where services were already inadequate. Families were impacted as married women entered the workforce in large numbers and once rationing was instituted, shortages of food, fuel, and raw materials added to the collective stress.[4] The questions in this section attest to the strains Americans were living with as they struggled with the war's impact.

During this period, Eleanor Roosevelt functioned as an informal government ombudsman, providing reassurance and clarity on a wide variety of issues, including military procedures and home front concerns. (For a brief time between September 1941 and February 1942, she actually held a government position as assistant director of the Office of Civilian Defense before congressional criticism drove her from office.) She also used "If You Ask Me" to build public support for the war effort, urging her readers to buy war bonds and resist the urge to hoard rationed or scarce items. On several occasions, she debunked rumors regarding the mental or physical health of returning veterans, draft regulations, and the presence of women in the military.

Much of this material may feel unfamiliar to contemporary readers who have never experienced the shortages and dislocations of war. Yet the fears and concerns these questions express are vivid reminders of war's effect on civilians.

Why wasn't the United States more prepared for war?

Because after the last war we made up our minds that we were never going to have another war. We taught our children at home and on the college campuses that war never settled affairs of state to anyone's satisfaction. We thoroughly convinced our young people of this, and they in turn convinced a great part of the country that we would never again have a period of war. Therefore, as we watched the rest of the world go to war, we simply insisted that staying at peace was something which we decided for ourselves and which had no relationship to the decisions of the rest of the world. Taking this attitude and feeling so secure, we quite naturally sent to Congress people who held the same opinion, and we upheld them in these opinions and would listen to no others. [MARCH 1942]

I have read many accounts of the events which took place in Washington on December 7, 1941, when Pearl Harbor was attacked, but I have never heard what happened in the White House that day. Could you tell us what happened when you and the President heard the news?*

My husband lunched upstairs in his study that day. We heard the news as we came out of the dining room downstairs, and when I reached the second floor I found that the President had already been informed. He was closeted almost immediately with state and military men, and the upstairs hall was lined with officials far into the night. The rest of us listened to the radio and tried to carry on our business. When I finally got to see my husband I found

---

* Eleanor Roosevelt's answer to this question is a summary of her initial account written soon after learning of the Pearl Harbor attacks. See "My Day," December 8, 1941, in The Eleanor Roosevelt Papers Digital Edition.

that, with all the shock and horror he felt, there was also that curious calm that comes to all of us when we know that something inevitable has to be faced and endured. [DECEMBER 1954]

Do you consider that the woman who stocks up now for the next two years on household and personal articles of which there is likely to be a shortage is a hoarder, or simply provident?

Any stocking up tends to make prices rise. I would advise buying as usual, and taking the chances that the average person has to take, if I wanted to sleep well at night. [DECEMBER 1941]

Do you think women are wrong to plan to have babies in these times?

Certainly not. If you have faith in the future of our civilization, you must be willing still to continue to do your share to populate the earth. [MARCH 1942]

Don't you think corsets should be classed as necessary, despite the rubber shortage?

No. I imagine we shall find some kind of substitute which will serve to keep us sylphlike. [MAY 1942]

Should we discourage children from playing war games?

We might wish to discourage them, but it would be utterly useless at the present time, so we might as well give in gracefully and try to see that when war games are played they teach the lessons which we wish our children to learn—fair play, magnanimity in victory, courage in defeat and no hatred of peoples. [AUGUST 1942]

Should I report a neighbor who is chiseling on gas and other rationing? I want to be patriotic, but I do not like being an informer.

I think it would be difficult for anyone to report a neighbor, and they should not do so unless they can produce absolute proof. If you are in an important position where you have a responsibility to the Government or to the community, then I think if you know of any citizen who is not living up to his obligation you should report it. [MARCH 1943]

Do you think expectant and nursing mothers should be given priority in food rationing?

I do. Even in Great Britain the young mother is given the same amount of milk a day as the children under fourteen, whereas other adults are left to go without if necessary. [MAY 1943]

How do you, as the mother of sons in active service, control your anxiety for them?

Largely by being so busy I have very little time to meet things before they happen. Many of our worries lie in anticipation of things which may never happen. When you have reached my age, life has taught you through discipline to meet situations when they must be met. [JUNE 1944]

Am I justified, when we are urged to avoid all unnecessary travel, in making a long and costly railroad journey to say good-by to my husband about to go overseas?

Certainly. That is why people are being urged not to travel unnecessarily. Nobody is urged to give up necessary journeys, and

I consider seeing your husband off and saying good-by before
he goes overseas an absolutely vital necessity, and nobody could
begrudge that to a wife. [AUGUST 1944]

*I hear people say, "Why buy bonds? Dollars won't be worth anything
after the war." What do you think?*

If bonds are worthless after the war, then any money you might
hoard would be worthless after the war, and anything you might
buy would be worthless because you would not be able to sell
it, and you cannot eat the things in the future which you buy at
present. By buying bonds you are preserving the future value of
your dollars, and therefore it is a very sensible thing for all of us
to do. [NOVEMBER 1942]

*Is it true that soldiers from the Midwestern states, which are normally
Republican, are sent into combat zones before soldiers from Democratic states?*

I have never heard anything so idiotic as your question. No soldier is
asked what his politics are, and they would be so mixed in the units
it would be utterly impossible to separate them. Anyone who believes
such a statement as this should go at once to a psychiatrist. [JULY 1943]

*Why are all our Christian boys drafted into the service while our Jewish
and colored boys are deferred and placed in good-paying defense jobs?*

That is just one of the lies which are circulated by our enemies.
Jews and colored boys are drafted into the services in exactly the
same proportion as any other, unless they happen to have an essential war job. If you will read the casualty lists and the list of

decorations for brave deeds, you will find many Jewish names. I know there are colored soldiers who have received medals for exceptional service, too, but there is no way of identifying them by their names. [OCTOBER 1943]

What do you think of women actually fighting, as they are reported to be doing in Russia?

When the time comes that women are needed in the fighting line, they will be found in the fighting line. They are evidently needed in Russia and they are doing what it is necessary for them to do. In the pioneer days of our own country, many a woman fought side by side with her husband; and if the need comes again, women will meet that need. [JULY 1942]

I have heard girls say they wouldn't think of joining the WAVES or WAACs* because they think that women who put on uniforms are aping men. What do you think of such a statement?

I think it is an utterly ridiculous statement. They are not aping men. They are wearing the kind of clothes which are suitable for the work they intend to do. If they do military work, they must of necessity wear military uniforms. If they work in a factory doing men's work, they will probably wear the type of garments which will make that work easier, and it is likely to be something like what the men wear. [JANUARY 1943]

---

* WAVES was the acronym for Women Accepted for Voluntary Emergency Service, the female branch of the U.S. Naval Reserve established in 1942. WAAC was the acronym for the Women's Army Auxiliary Corps, which was created in 1942 as an auxiliary to the U.S. Army.

Don't you think the stories about WAAC immorality are terribly unfair, considering the fact that every time women take over new fields where men are, the charge of increasing immorality is invariably made?[5]

I am assured by the authorities that the morality among the WAACs is very high. These girls have stricter supervision than any other group of girls in the country, and they are serious-minded young women who have volunteered for a war job.

This rumor about immorality went the rounds in Great Britain and in Canada when women started to replace men, and it looks to me very much like Axis-inspired propaganda. We have now in the WAAC the equivalent of four divisions, and when it is up to the authorized strength we will have the equal of ten divisions of men. When you realize that the Axis would do anything to prevent our building up a force of women which will release that many men for actual combat, it is easy to understand that the Axis would be pleased if these rumors were to affect our enlistments. Many innocent people repeat this rumor and are thereby playing Hitler's game and doing what he would like to have us do—namely, to discredit our women. [AUGUST 1943]

Why are the Allied countries not rescuing the Jewish people in Nazi-dominated countries before they are entirely destroyed?

Most of the Allied countries in Europe, with the exception of Great Britain and Russia, are in the possession of the Nazis. Sweden, Switzerland, Turkey and a few others are neutrals, but the others are either under the domination of the Nazis or co-operating with them, so it seems to me that it is fairly obvious that there is no way to rescue the Jewish people except by winning the war.*

Everything that can be done by diplomatic representations and expressions of government disapproval of the actions of the Nazis has already been done. [MARCH 1944]

Are you supporting several child refugees?

I subscribe every month to the support in Great Britain of two refugee children. I do this through the Foster Parents Plan for War Children, Inc. I felt, however, that if I contributed to the care of children abroad I wanted, at the same time, to help some unfortunate child in my own country, and so I pay the board of one needy American child. I find that it costs almost as much to do that here for one child as it does to help three children in Great Britain! [APRIL 1944]

---

* Eleanor Roosevelt's reply to this question reflected the prevailing U.S. diplomatic and military policy that winning the war was the best way to save the Jews of Europe. Her own view was quite different. Since the mid-1930s she had worked to educate American public opinion about the Jews' plight. During the prewar period, she had also supported pro-immigration groups and legislation and lobbied F.D.R. and Congress to allow Jewish refugees to enter the United States. After America entered World War II, she walked a fine line, continuing her activism while upholding the government's policy. Shortly before this question appeared in print, the government's policy changed with the establishment of the War Refugee Board which was charged with rescuing and aiding Jews and other Nazi-persecuted minorities.[6]

With what the Germans, Japanese and Italians are trying to do to the democracies of the world—especially our United States—do you really mean you would permit your children to number among their friends any Germans, Japanese or Italians?

I certainly do. How are we going to live in peace in the world of the future if we cannot be friends ourselves with Germans, Japanese or Italians? I have friends of all those nationalities; some of them have fled their own countries because they were in disagreement with the policies of the governments of those countries. I imagine there are many people still in those countries who are suffering because they do not agree with what their governments are doing. If we take the attitude that we can never be friends with people of these nationalities, our chance for a peaceful world in the future is slim indeed. [SEPTEMBER 1942]

How do you think our boys who have gone to war and risked their lives should treat conscientious objectors after the war?

I should think that the boys who go through the war, and who believe in what they are doing, would have a respect for a conscientious objector who had an equally strong belief that he should not kill other people.

We have put these conscientious objectors to work in this war. They are clamoring for more dangerous work. Some of them are already doing work which requires great courage, but not the taking of another man's life. It would certainly seem a curious thing for me if a boy were not able to understand, having had deep convictions himself, that other people have a right to equally deep convictions and that they should be respected. [AUGUST 1942]

Do you think monuments commemorating war heroes waste thousands of dollars better spent for housing, or recreational and educational facilities dedicated to community heroes?

My own personal preference is a monument which will be of value to the living. Therefore, I would prefer one in any community to include recreational and educational facilities. However, in the case of war heroes, I think the feelings of the immediate families should be considered, and if they feel this type of monument does not bring home to the people of the community sufficiently poignantly what their men have done, then the more traditional monuments which you see in towns and villages as war memorials of the past should certainly be erected. The object is to give all solace possible to those who have lost men. [OCTOBER 1944]

Do you approve of the return at Government expense of the bodies of servicemen who were buried overseas?

Naturally if the bodies are going to be brought home they must be brought home by the Government. One does not approve or disapprove of this. Different people feel differently about it. I happen to belong to a family whose members have always wanted to be buried where they died, but I know many people who feel differently and I think it is a question for individuals and their families to decide. [AUGUST 1948]

Do you think it a sound principle of justice to try the so-called "war criminals" for acts that were not technically illegal under either German or Japanese or international law at the time they were committed?

Yes, I think it is a sound principle of justice to try people for acts they committed, whether they were technically illegal or not at the time. I realize that this is not the procedure usually adhered to by the courts, but I have always felt that that was one of the unfortunate ways in which justice sometimes miscarries even in domestic issues. [MARCH 1946]

Why do you so strongly advocate a year of training to discipline the youth of our nation?

I do not advocate a year of training to discipline the youth of our nation. Discipline is a by-product. I think we are likely to have a year of military training, and I would prefer not to have it completely military because I feel that all that can be learned along military lines can probably be taught either in three months or in a certain number of hours each day over the period of a year. Much might be given our boys and girls during this year which would be valuable to them for the rest of their lives and which would have for its main objective increasing the understanding and responsibility for citizenship in a democracy. [MARCH 1945]

What, specifically, can we do now to help bring about a just and lasting peace at the end of this war?

Face the fact that we are going to have to make a world-wide economic adjustment. That we are going to have to be willing to accept much responsibility for the world as a whole. That it is going to mean plenty of work for all of us. Inform ourselves on economic and historical questions dealing with the world as a whole. Prepare to be just to all nations and not allow ourselves to seek any personal advantage. Be thinking now about the machinery we are willing to accept in order to have some method of adjustment in the future, and take some responsibility now in the choice of public servants so that when the time comes to make peace we will feel that in both the executive and the legislative bodies we have people who can be trusted to formulate the kind of peace that we are willing to back. [APRIL 1942]

What is your personal postwar plan?

My personal postwar plan is to try to be as good a citizen as possible in private life, and to work as hard as I can at work which I enjoy. To have more time for my own interests and to spend with people whom I love. [JUNE 1944]

Relations between the United States and the Soviet Union disintegrated quickly after the end of World War II. A succession of events including the Berlin Airlift (1948), the consolidation of Soviet satellite regimes in Eastern Europe, the successful test of the Soviet Union's first atomic bomb (1949), the end of the Chinese civil war and the creation of the People's Republic of China (1949), and the outbreak of the Korean War (1950) convinced many Americans that World War III was only a matter of time. The United States' successful test of a hydrogen bomb in 1954, and the failure of a 1956 anti-communist revolt in Hungary only heightened the tense state of international affairs.

As one of the few Americans who interacted with Soviet officials through her work with the United Nations and later through her travels in the Soviet Union (she visited twice, first in 1957 and again in 1958), Eleanor Roosevelt was well-placed to deal with her readers' concerns. While she did not minimize the dangers and difficulties of dealing with Soviet diplomats (in 1947 she titled a *Look* magazine article "The Russians Are Tough"), she refused to subscribe to the hard-line view that nothing could be gained from negotiations with them. She encouraged Americans to meet the Soviet threat with strength and goodwill while bolstering democracy at home and abroad, particularly in the emerging nations of the Third World. Communism, she believed, would only triumph if democracies failed to secure justice, equality, and an adequate standard of life for all their people.[7]

Is there anything we can do to convince other countries that not all Americans are money grabbers, strikers and growing isolationists?

Yes. There is a great deal we can do. We can devote ourselves to being good citizens in our communities and to creating public opinion which will make our own community a truly democratic one. If this is so, there will be less isolationism, fewer strikes and the money grabbers will not be very popular. Each one of us can do no more than his share in his own community, but that he must do, or the community will not be part of the whole structure which we hope will be a better world. [SEPTEMBER 1946]

What, in the eyes of the world, do you think is our most serious national fault?

Complacency and a lack of recognition of the contributions made by other nations in the areas in which they have something to offer. [NOVEMBER 1959]

I have heard it said before that, in the eyes of the rest of the world, the American wish for popularity, our desire to have everyone "love" us, makes us weak and vacillating. Do you think there is any truth in this statement?

I think we have to realize that it is much more important to have the respect of other peoples than to have their love. We sometimes seem to believe that just because we give material things to aid others, they must of necessity like us. This is, of course, untrue. Liking comes when a sufficient number of people know one another and have real understanding and enjoyment in their contacts. But in dealing with other nations, our government should primarily seek to command respect for the United States. [SEPTEMBER 1962]

My only child is almost three, and ordinarily I would consider having another in the next year, but I am afraid to bring a baby into this world with its present uncertainties. When I read about the dreadful things that can happen I become actually ill with fear of what our future may be. Have you any advice for me?

Yes. Stop being afraid. Suppose our great-grandmothers had been afraid to leave Virginia, for instance, and journey westward; this country would never have been settled—and they faced as many uncertainties and unknowns as we do today. You will ruin your child of three if you live under a cloud of fear, and you will ruin yourself as a citizen, and your own happiness and that of your family, if you do not learn to face whatever comes with courage. If you haven't got courage, make believe you have it and that will help you to acquire it. [OCTOBER 1948]

What do you think is the greatest single cause of misunderstanding between the nations of the world, both great and small?

Fear. [JUNE 1946]

I would like your opinion on the following question: Do occupational forces teach democracy?

I suppose what you mean is: "Do our armies of occupation teach democracy?" That all depends upon how well our armies understand democracy. I am afraid young men in armies of occupation are far from understanding the real underlying principles of democracy or wanting to practice these principles as a way of life. A few do understand and are genuinely devoted to democratic ideals, both in government and in their way of living. When that is the case, they are without question increasing the knowledge of democracy wherever they are stationed. [JULY 1946]

What is your opinion of the North Atlantic Pact? Is it a wise move, or are we just looking for trouble?

The North Atlantic Pact is a wise move, I think. At the present there is no force within the United Nations because, until the U.S.S.R. and the U.S.A. come to some kind of understanding on atomic energy, there can be no force set up within the United Nations. Therefore some kind of strength to give security to the smaller nations must be set up. The North Atlantic Pact assures greater security to all those nations belonging to it, since it is a defensive pact and it agrees that if any nation is threatened with aggression the other member nations will immediately consult and take such steps as seem necessary. This should help us to safeguard the peace of the world. [JULY 1949]

Nikita Khrushchev (1894–1971) came to power in the Soviet Union following the death of Premier Joseph Stalin in 1953. Domestically he presided over a period of comparative political openness, ending his predecessor's reign of terror and freeing many political prisoners. He also reoriented Soviet industry toward the production of consumer goods rather than military weapons. A firm believer in the inevitable triumph of communism over capitalism, Khrushchev nevertheless pursued a policy of peaceful coexistence with noncommunist countries, including the United States. However, his penchant for belligerent gestures and inflammatory rhetoric encouraged the belief that he had warlike intentions. Eleanor Roosevelt was one of the few westerners who had firsthand contact with the Soviet leader, having interviewed him during her 1957 visit to the Soviet Union. Two years later they met again when he visited the United States.[8]

Do you think Khrushchev is telling the truth when he says he doesn't want war? If he is and no one wants war, what are we afraid of?

Yes. He knows the power of destruction and knows that, in all probability, destruction could not be limited. But this does not mean there is not grave danger of having war either accidentally or through some irresponsible action—not always by the chief of a state. We are afraid of such an accidental war, and also of being conquered by Communism through nonmilitary means. [JANUARY 1961]

What, if anything, do you believe the Americans and Russians have in common?

Many things. They are all human beings, and all human beings love and hate, are hungry or satisfied, tired or rested, ill or well, and all human beings have the same desire to live in peace, to have just and fair government which allows them to develop to the best of their ability. The differences come in the circumstances which surround human beings, and that is immediately where you come to the differences between the Americans and Russians. [OCTOBER 1953]

Why do you think the Russians got ahead of us in developing satellites?

In a democracy you have to rely on leadership from the administration plus financing from Congress, whereas in Russia the central government both makes the decisions and carries them out. The Russians are extremely research-minded and they put a great deal of money and effort into it, which is one reason, I think, that they may be moving ahead faster than we are in this area. It is not that we can't move ahead faster, it is that as a people we do not seem to realize how essential scientific research is and Congress hesitates to appropriate money for things it is not sure the voters want. [FEBRUARY 1958]

Boris Pasternak (1890–1960), a Russian poet, novelist, and translator caused an international furor when *Doctor Zhivago*, his novel set during the Bolshevik Revolution, was published in the west and won him the 1958 Nobel Prize for Literature. The Soviets, who had not published the book because it "libeled" the revolution, refused to allow him to accept the award and started a campaign against him. Pasternak lost his job as a translator and there were public calls for his deportation. Pasternak wrote the Soviet government declining the award and begging to be allowed to stay, saying, "Leaving the motherland will equal death for me." The authorities allowed him to remain, and he lived in Russia until his death. In 1988, the Soviets finally permitted *Doctor Zhivago* to be published in Russian.[9]

Do you believe Boris Pasternak,* the author of Doctor Zhivago, *can be sincere in his criticisms of Russia if he begged the Government to let him stay there?*

Certainly he can. He loves his country and wants to live there. He does not want to leave the place where his friends and his family are. We criticize the United States, but we do not want to be put out of our country for doing so. I doubt that Mr. Pasternak realized how much furor his book would arouse outside Russia.

[MARCH 1959]

* Eleanor Roosevelt wrote Nikita Khrushchev to protest the Soviet Union's refusal to let Pasternak accept the Nobel Prize for Literature.

How does the H-bomb alter the chances for world peace?

I think the H-bomb helps to remove the chances of war, because our scientists recognize that the H-bomb may be a completely destructive weapon. That means, of course, that the U.S.S.R. scientists also know this, and I have an idea that the Politburo is quite as anxious to continue to have a world in which to live as we are.

If experimentation with the H-bomb means possible destruction, it may prove the greatest incentive to keeping us at peace. I think this might be emphasized more than it is at the present time. [JUNE 1950]

What in your opinion would be the most serious problems if New York City should suffer an atom-bomb attack?

I do not think I know enough to answer this question, but, judging from what happened in Japan, I would think the organization of medical relief, fire fighting and the discovery and use of anything which would reduce radioactivity would be the most urgent problems. After that would come the provision of food and shelter and the removal of people as far as possible from the radioactive areas. [OCTOBER 1950] (Question from Vincent Impellitteri,* the acting mayor of New York.)

* Vincent Impellitteri (1900–1987), a New York City lawyer, politician, and president of the city council (1946–1950), became acting mayor in 1950 following the resignation of William O'Dwyer, who left to become U.S. ambassador to Mexico. Impellitteri then won a special election to serve the remaining three years of O'Dwyer's term. He ran for re-election in 1953 but was defeated. He subsequently became a criminal court judge.[10]

I am in the eighth grade, and my class is having a debate on the question why don't we just drop the atomic bomb on Russia before they drop it on us? I would appreciate it if you would answer my letter.

There is a very simple answer to your question. The country that uses an atom bomb in an undeclared war will be the most hated country in the world, and no one in that country will ever sleep without fear of reprisal. A great deal of destruction can be brought about, and a great many innocent people can be killed by dropping a bomb on Russia, but a country such as the Soviet Union, where the people are scattered over the land, would not suffer as we would here in the United States, with our population so highly concentrated in large cities. [FEBRUARY 1951]

How can I reassure my children about the atom bomb? They've heard so much about it on the radio and at school, it seems to be an obsession with them.

You can only free children from fear by developing a philosophy yourself which is free from fear, and by explaining to the children that to live in fear is worse than actually to face the danger of extinction. If you can give them a trust in God, that is the one sure way of being able to meet all the uncertainties of existence. [MARCH 1951]

My five-and-a-half-year-old son asked me, "Mother, what makes war?" I don't know what to say. How can you answer a small boy like this in terms he'll understand?

I think the only thing to do is to explain to him that nations are not very different from individual people. He knows there are times when he quarrels with his playmates. Make him analyze what brings about those quarrels and he will soon understand how, on the national level, wars occur in the world. [JULY 1951]

Looking back on it, Mrs. Roosevelt, would you say that the United States was morally justified in dropping the A-bomb on the Japanese people?

I feel quite sure that if I had been President Truman I would have made the same decision he made. I wish very much that as a nation we had never been placed in a position where such a choice had to be made, and I hope very much that never again will a weapon of this kind be used by any nation. [DECEMBER 1955]

Should federal or state governments build bomb shelters for everyone? If there couldn't be enough for everyone, should there be none?

I think it is nonsense to build bomb shelters. It is quite evident, from all we are told about modern nuclear weapons, that the shelters would be useless. We had better bend our efforts to preventing nuclear war and not worry about how we can preserve our own skins. I do not approve of individuals' building shelters, and I would consider it a waste of government money to build them for public use. [NOVEMBER 1960]

In his 1946 speech at Westminster College in Fulton, Missouri, former British prime minister Winston Churchill said that an "Iron Curtain" of Soviet influence and domination had "descended across" the countries of Eastern Europe cutting them off from the rest of Europe. While he did not believe the Soviets wanted war, Churchill thought they sought "the fruits of war and the indefinite expansion of their powers and doctrines." To prevent such an outcome and safeguard the West's liberties he called for an Anglo-American alliance that some observers interpreted as military in nature. Eleanor Roosevelt disagreed with Churchill, fearing that such an alliance would undermine the nascent United Nations and further antagonize the Soviet Union while embroiling the United States in age-old European conflicts. She made her opposition public by writing that Churchill's proposal did not "differ very greatly from the old balance of power politics" that had been "going on in Europe for hundreds of years." She argued that the United Nations, with its emphasis on discussion, collective security, and equal representation for all nations regardless of size, offered a better chance for peace. Churchill subsequently visited Eleanor at Hyde Park where she allegedly told the former prime minister that he was "desecrating the ideals for which [her] husband gave his life." She denied making that statement once in her newspaper column and again in the following exchange.[11]

Is it true that at the time of Winston Churchill's speech at Fulton, Missouri, you reprimanded him? It was reported over the radio that you told Mr. Churchill that he had torn down all that your husband had believed in and worked for regarding Russia.

Of course it is utterly untrue that I reprimanded Mr. Churchill. It would hardly be fitting for me to do so. If Mr. Churchill had asked me for my opinion on his Fulton, Missouri, speech, I could not have told him what my husband would have felt about it, because I do not believe in trying to say what people who are not here to speak for themselves might have said. I certainly would have told Mr. Churchill, if I had been asked, that I thought it an unwise speech to make, and that I regretted it. He probably knew what my attitude would be if he even bothered to think about it when he made the speech. Therefore it would seem to me that offering any comment without invitation would have been foolish. [JUNE 1948]

Like many others nowadays, the thought of what an atom war could do to our world often comes to my mind. But, like most others, I push it to the back of my consciousness with the excuse that there is nothing that I myself can do about it. Is there anything really which the common man can do?

Yes, there is a great deal that the common man can do. We can work for peace. Even during the war some of our leaders were thinking about how to establish a unity among nations after the war which might prevent future wars. The machinery was set in motion first to write a charter which could be agreed to by many nations. At present fifty-one nations have agreed to that charter and in London, on January 10, they sent delegates actually to set up the machinery to implement that charter. That is now done. The permanent home of this organization will be in this country and under it many undertakings will begin which we hope will lead us to a peaceful world.

However, this will only be possible if the peoples of the various nations keep their interest alive and work to the best of their ability under the organization, whether it is a health organization, or an educational organization, or a labor organization, or any of the other numerous organizations which create the ties among peoples that make them want to work together and not to fight each other.

You and I, as ordinary citizens, can work for these various undertakings and, above everything else, we can create public opinion and make it favorable to cooperation. When one has seen Europe or the Pacific and understands what modern war does to countries and peoples, one can fully realize, I think, that our future existence depends on making the UNO* a vital instrument for peace. [MAY 1946]

I am a girl of eighteen and worried by my father. He tells me that my ideals about international responsibility for peace are just "book theories," that there has always been war and always will be. He says that now, like the last time, we are going back to isolation. Must this be inevitable? Is he right? If you believe, as I do, that people and nations can change, what would you suggest that I, as one too young to vote, can do about it?

I do not think it is inevitable that we make the same mistakes over and over again. As you read history, you feel that human beings are slow to learn and that our steps forward are often accompa-

---

* In its earliest years, the United Nations was often referred to as the United Nations Organization (UNO).

nied by waves of retrogression. There is nothing to do, however, but to work for the things in which you believe. You may not be able to vote now, but you can work in the organizations that are trying to bring about the things that you think are right; and in your own life, you can live as you think people should live to bring peace and better citizenship into the world. You will then be prepared to vote more intelligently and to be a better citizen. [OCTOBER 1946]

I am in the sixth grade. What can I do to make the world more peaceful?

You can learn to live harmoniously with people of your own age even though they might be of different races and different religions. If you do that you will be preparing your generation to live better and more peacefully in the world as a whole. [APRIL 1953]

Do you see any value in the various women's groups' "marching for peace" outside the White House and UN? We certainly all want peace, but this seems as negative and pacifist as Britain's "Ban the Bomb" sit-ins.

The average person has a sense of frustration because he can think of no way to express to his government or to the world at large his desire for peaceful solutions to the difficulties that confront us. The demonstrations you mention are important if only because they dramatize the lack of more useful ways for people to show their devotion to the cause of peace. [MAY 1962]

Although Eleanor Roosevelt considered the founding of the United Nations the most significant accomplishment of the twentieth century, and her work in the creation and passage of the Universal Declaration of Human Rights (U.D.H.R.) the most important achievement of her career, the editors and/or readers of "If You Ask Me" apparently did not always share her passion for the organization. The number of questions pertaining to the U.N. is small compared with the number dealing with World War II, the Cold War, or such personal concerns as marriage and child-rearing.[12]

The lack of interest may have been due to the newness of the organization, which met formally for the first time in January 1946. Some Americans, remembering the failure of the League of Nations in the 1930s, did not think the U.N. would survive the rigors of the Cold War. Others saw it as the harbinger of world government and a threat to U.S. sovereignty.

To Eleanor, the U.N. was "machinery for the furtherance of peace," a mechanism by which all nations large or small could come together to discuss their problems and devise solutions. Making that machinery work, she believed, would require a concerted effort on the part of citizens and their governments. "We should remember that the United Nations is not a cure-all," she told the audience at the 1952 Democratic National Convention. "It is only an instrument capable of effective action when its members have a will to make it work. It cannot be any better than the individual nations are."[13]

Eleanor's support for the U.N. gave the international organization much-needed credibility in the early years of its existence. As a U.S. delegate from 1946–1952, she consistently publicized the organization's work in her columns, radio broadcasts, and speeches. After Dwight D. Eisenhower declined to re-appoint her to the U.S. delegation, she volunteered at the American Association for the United Nations, a nonpartisan organization that encouraged support for the U.N. In that capacity she traveled thousands of miles each year to foster recognition of the U.N. and its work while refuting its opponents' claims that it was a communist-front organization. Reappointed to the U.S. delegation in 1961, she served briefly before ill health forced her to become, at her own request, a special advisor to the group. After her death, her close friend and colleague U.S. ambassador to the U.N. Adlai Stevenson recalled her impact, saying, she "had breathed life into the United Nations."[14]

As a delegate to the UNO, will you be guided under any circumstances by your individual judgment of what is right, or under certain possible circumstances by the principle, "My country: may it ever be right; but right or wrong, my country"?

I will, of course, as a delegate to the UNO have to abide by whatever rules are set up within our delegation to govern procedures. Where decisions of policy are made within the delegation, I will try to represent the people. I know, of course, that my feeling of what should be done or of what people want may be wrong, but I would certainly try to work for what I thought represented the major good of the world as a whole. I will try to think at all times of ultimate objectives rather than of the narrower and more immediate aspects of any question that comes up as it affects my own or any other individual country.

I will do this because I believe so firmly that the good of all people in the future must be paramount in order to make it possible for any one of us to live and be free and happy on this globe.

"My country: may it ever be right; but my country, right or wrong" is a very good precept for men in our military services, since they are under the orders of Congress and their Commander-in-Chief and really have very little opportunity to form the policies of the nation. They are practically obligated, once a decision is made, to carry it out. For the rest of us, however, who have an obligation to take part in the forming of policies, I think we should make every possible effort to fight for the things which we believe are right, making it clear to the people why we hold our beliefs, thus creating public opinion. The majority must rule, but minorities sometimes become majorities, and full knowledge for the people is the only way that we, in a democracy, can be truly representative of the will of the people. [MARCH 1946]

Do you consider your work with the United Nations as a "sacrifice"? If so, what would you rather do than this?

I cannot remember saying anything which would give the impression that I consider my work with the United Nations a sacrifice. There are times when that work does entail sacrifice of time and comfort, but so does all worth-while work. I consider it an honor to be allowed to work with the United Nations; to have the confidence of those who appoint me and of the majority of the legislative group that has to ratify the appointment. If I am able to keep the respect and good will of those with whom I work, I shall be extremely grateful. [SEPTEMBER 1948]

Don't you think that today, more than ever, we need a universal language, so that representatives of all nations can communicate readily with one another? For example, Esperanto. It seems to me the UN should do something about this.

I am afraid I am not very sympathetic with the idea of a synthetic language when, as far as I can see, more and more people are making English their second language. The UN is in an English-speaking country, and representatives from other countries learn English, some of them very rapidly. All over the world, English is becoming the second language taught in schools. I think that having one language in which all can communicate is valuable, but it does not take the place of communicating with people in their own tongues. Therefore, learning as many languages as possible is always important for people who are interested in world affairs and in promoting better understanding among peoples. [FEBRUARY 1960]

Our ninth grade would appreciate it very much if you would tell us what was your most thrilling experience at the United Nations.

My most thrilling experience was the final adoption of the Universal Declaration of Human Rights, which was the culmination of very hard work and I think an important step in international development. [JUNE 1955]

The Russian delegates to the U.N. seem very cold and inhuman in their public appearances, but I understand that in private many of them are very pleasant and amusing. Have you found this to be true? Which ones especially?

I have had very few occasions on which to discover whether any of the Russian delegates are different in private from what they are in public. A few of them have dined with me, usually with an interpreter sitting behind their chairs. A few have spent evenings in my sitting room and on such occasions have been pleasant guests. They have always been courteous when they came, but they are nearly always impersonal and always very guarded in their remarks, never forgetting that they are government representatives and cannot speak in a personal capacity. [SEPTEMBER 1951]

Our newspaper published an amazing picture of you, smiling, all sweetness and light, as you shook hands with Russia's Ambassador Gromyko at the recent opening of the U.N. Who are you kidding?

I did not know I was kidding anyone. I was preserving the amenities. When you shake hands you usually smile. To reach our seats in the General Assembly we have to pass directly in front of the Russian and the United Kingdom delegates. I have known

Mr. Gromyko for a long time, and the newspaper photographers—who are always on the alert—insisted on taking the photograph.

I believe as long as we serve in the General Assembly, or anywhere in the United Nations, we must be polite to one another, and we must be able to talk to one another in the hope that someday this bridge will be used for the benefit of a peaceful settlement of our difficulties. [MARCH 1953]

Chapter 10

HEALTH AND AGING

MEDICAL ADVANCES OVER the course of Eleanor Roo-sevelt's lifetime, including the discovery of insulin, antibiotics, and a groundbreaking vaccine for polio, substantially increased the number of older Americans. Between 1930 and 1957, this segment of the population more than doubled, giving rise to reader questions about elder care and meaning.[1]

When it came to aging, Eleanor had certain fixed principles. Retirement should not be automatic. Older people should maintain their independence as long as possible. They should remain active and cultivate their own interests. They should avoid living with their offspring and their families unless it was financially necessary. Above all they should not interfere with their children's marriages or their grandchildren's upbringing financially or otherwise.[2]

Eleanor's views on aging stemmed from her own experience. She knew what it was to live with an interfering mother-in-law. She had watched her grandmother Mary Ludlow Hall fail to develop any interests outside her family. Widowed at sixty-one, Eleanor had had to reinvent herself after leaving the White House.[3]

Believing as she did that "life must be lived," Eleanor was her own best example. "I could not, at any age, be content to take my place in a corner by the fireside and simply look on," she told an interviewer the year before she died. And she didn't. The last seventeen years of her life were among her most productive as she combined the roles of journalist, diplomat, politician, activist, and teacher with that of matriarch of a large extended family.[4]

Eleanor's enthusiasm for living and her often-hectic schedule amazed her contemporaries who marveled at her stamina but wondered what lay behind it: Had she ever experienced moments of depression or doubt? Had she ever considered suicide? Her answer to both questions was yes, but she had used work, her interest in others, and self-discipline to combat them. That is not to say that she thought therapy was unnecessary or useless. On the contrary, she thought mental illness was just as valid as physical illness and should be treated accordingly—a position that put her at odds with many of her contemporaries who thought difficult emotional or mental problems should be ignored rather than discussed.

As for the issue of health care generally, she believed that a system of national health care would benefit young and old and result in better health for all Americans and she favored the expansion of social security to cover these costs for elderly Americans so their children would not be burdened with those expenses while trying to establish their own lives and families.

While she enjoyed excellent health (she once described herself as "a tough old girl"), Eleanor was philosophic about the inevitability of old age and determined to avoid the self-absorption it often encouraged.[5] Until her final illness she lived in the present and worked for the future without worrying about what lay ahead. When death came she would face it the same way she had lived: "You have to accept whatever comes and the only important thing is that you meet it with courage and with the best that you have to give," she told an interviewer. Rejecting life was the only nonnegotiable. "One must never, for whatever reason, turn his back on life."[6] In a society that paradoxically exalts youth while the population over age sixty-five explodes, where age discrimination is common, and retirement if and when it comes can sometimes look like the end, Eleanor's words and her example are a bracing reminder that life is worth living at any age, and time is too precious to waste.

Most women fib about their age at some time, but I never had until now. Recently, when applying for a job, I was discriminated against because of my age. My prospective employer was extremely pleased with my work until I told him my age, and then his whole attitude changed. I decided not to be so frank in the future, but my husband argues that the Social Security Board will catch up with me and notify my employer of the discrepancy between his reports and their files. Is this true?

I think any employer who is satisfied with your work and then, when you tell him your age, loses interest in the work which you have done, is a pretty weak reed on which to lean for continuous employment. However, if your worry is just about the Social Security Board, you can be entirely honest with them, since I understand that they never divulge any person's age to any employer. However, you should be sure to tell the Social Security Board the truth because I think it might be serious if the records were not accurate. [MAY 1946]

We have been having an argument over what age is called middle age and what is old age. I would very much like your opinion.

Age is a matter of the mind as well as of the body. I have known people old in years who were yet young in their outlook on life and in some ways managed even to keep their bodies young by their mental processes.

Ordinarily, old age is supposed to begin at sixty. After that you are more or less living on borrowed time, and after seventy most people count each year as an unusual gift. [DECEMBER 1947]

Would you mind giving me your definition of a mature person?

A mature person is one who does not think only in absolutes, who is able to be objective even when deeply stirred emotionally, who has learned that there is both good and bad in all people and in all things, and who walks humbly and deals charitably with the circumstances of life, knowing that in this world no one is all-knowing and therefore all of us need both love and charity. [OCTOBER 1953]

Do you think it's fair to retire people at 65? The average length of life increases all the time, but the retirement age stays the same. It doesn't make any sense to me.

No, I do not think people should be retired automatically at 65. Those who are able to go on working I think should go on, even though undergoing periodic physical examinations. If it would be better for them to retire and do some other kind of work, I think they should be given the opportunity for training and be put into that other kind of work. To leave people with no work when the expectancy of life has much increased, I agree with you, makes very little sense. [SEPTEMBER 1951]

Don't you think it would help reduce automobile accidents if there were an age limit beyond which people were not allowed to drive?

An age limit does not seem very sensible, but a periodic examination to make sure that an older person can still pass the driving tests would seem to me a wise safeguard. Many of our accidents occur with young people because of failure in judgment, a more reckless attitude, and a perfectly natural affinity to speed. I have never looked into the statistics, but I would be surprised if people over fifty had more accidents than people under fifty. [JUNE 1959]

It has long been recognized that one of the great burdens of aging is a feeling of uselessness. Have you any suggestions for ways in which an older woman of average health and resources can make herself the most useful to her family and to her community?

I think an older woman living alone has a great opportunity for usefulness to her family and to her community. She can offer experienced help with children in time of illness. She can work as a volunteer or even as a paid worker in many community activities, with both young and old. She has the time and experience that are needed to work in organizations, and if she has the health and enough money to live on, she can give herself freely. There are many things that need to be done in any community, if all you are asking for is to be useful. [MARCH 1962]

My husband's mother is coming to live with us. She has lived by herself far away for a long time and has been extremely unhappy and lonely. We have had an unusually happy marriage and I have a happy disposition, but when she's here I find it is all I can do to keep from displaying ill temper and being depressed. She and my husband seem so happy together and I feel like a wet blanket and finally lose confidence in myself. My husband is a fine man with a strong character. I have three lovely sons—one a small baby. I want to do a good job in bringing up our children. How can I learn to relax and to have positive thinking about this? Is there anything I can read that will help?

If I were you, I would have a talk with your mother-in-law and with your husband, together or separately, as you find easier, but I would tell them both the same things: namely, that somehow a way must be found in which you can be included in the pleasures they find in their mutual companionship. You must, of course, make an effort to be companionable. If your mother-in-law is going to live with you, definite rules as regards the children should be decided on. You must have the final say-so, and there must be no effort to sabotage your discipline or your position with the children. Grandmothers can be a great help, but they can also be a heart-rending burden to their daughters-in-law, and only honesty between all concerned can save that situation. Honestly talking over things and not repressing your feelings, but making an effort to be kind and spontaneous in your contacts, will, I hope, bring you success. [MAY 1948]

If for financial or physical reasons you were not able to live independently now, would you move in with one of your children or would you consider some kind of residence for older people? At 78 I am no longer strong enough to run my own house. I hate to burden my daughter and her husband, who have three small children, but I also hate the thought of an "old-age" home.

I have seen some very delightful homes where I should be entirely contented to go and live if I were no longer able to live in my own home. It is a mistake, I think, for older people to move in with a young family. I know it was frequently done years ago. Having Grandmother in the house was often useful and valuable for the children, but modern life is lived in smaller quarters, it is more hurried and less leisurely, and I think it is harder for different generations to adjust to each other. Personally, therefore, I should prefer to try to find a home in which I felt I could have some privacy and live contentedly during my old age. [MAY 1955]

How do you personally feel free medical aid for the aged should be handled?

I feel very strongly that this should be compulsory and automatic under Social Security, and I also feel that Social Security should increase its coverage so that more people are included in its benefits. Medical care for the aged is as important to young people as it is to old. If Social Security does not cover this care, young people are obliged to take on the burden of their parents' medical bills. [FEBRUARY 1961]

Do you think 67 is too old for someone to get psychoanalyzed?

I don't suppose one is ever too old for anything, but if at 67 you have not learned to know yourself, it is a little hard for me to believe that anyone else can help you to do so. I would certainly advise you to do it, however, if you really feel it will help. [AUGUST 1956]

Do you approve of psychoanalysis?

I certainly do approve of psychoanalysis when it is needed and when it is practiced by responsible, well-trained people. [AUGUST 1959]

The Mental Health Association claims that one in ten of our citizens is mentally ill. To what do you attribute this increase of mental illness in this country?

Personally, I doubt that there has been any increase in mental illness—only an increase in our awareness of it. When I was a girl, I remember many, many people who suffered from such problems. If their cases were not severe, they were called "eccentrics" or "not quite right"; if they suffered from more serious problems, they were literally confined to attic rooms. Many family circles included one such member; but since they were considered a disgrace, they were kept out of sight and never discussed outside the family. Today, happily, we are far more enlightened and understand that such people are suffering from a disease that can be treated. Since we are generally more open about mental illness, I believe it simply appears to be more prevalent than formerly. [OCTOBER 1962]

Are you ever lonely? If so, how do you dispel the blues?

I can never remember being lonely, but if I feel depressed I go to work. Work is always an antidote for depression, and loneliness is just one of the manifestations of this frame of mind or state of soul which is the lot of all human beings. [OCTOBER 1944]

How do you keep from worrying? You must have many more worries than most of us, yet worry never seems to get you down.

Everyone living, of course, has worries; and if they have many people whom they care about, naturally they are concerned about them and their worries. But I learned many years ago that worry which did not lead to being able to do something was useless. The best way to alleviate worry is to do all you can. [JULY 1950]

How do you avoid distraction, depression and the total inability to work that occasionally besets most people in this difficult life?

As far as distraction goes, I learned how to concentrate many years ago by having to read in a living room where my boisterous children were playing. I have never found that depression took such a hold on me that I was not able to work. In fact, concentration on work and being interested in it is the best antidote I know for depression. I think it requires self-discipline, and that has been more or less forced on me ever since I was a child, so it has become a rather settled habit by now. [JUNE 1954]

What is your formula for getting ahold of your emotions in a critical time like your husband's death, for example, and facing things calmly?

I think any great calamity always brings with it a certain numbness which makes it easier to be calm. The difficulty, really, is later when the reaction sets in. At the time of a great blow it is almost impossible to take in just what has happened, and so you turn your attention to minutiae—little things which have to be done and which keep you on an even keel. One does, of course, draw unconsciously upon the disciplines and habits built up through a lifetime. If one has learned to control emotions, then even when the reaction sets in it is possible to think of other people instead of oneself and to meet the obligations of the time and the situation. [DECEMBER 1957]

Has the thought of suicide entered your mind at any period in your life? What kept you from doing it?

I doubt that any human being goes through life without at some time feeling it might be better if things came to an end, but almost always something tells you that this is an impossible solution. Usually suicide would harm other people or it would leave greater burdens on other people's shoulders. I doubt that I ever really seriously contemplated it, though I must admit that like everyone else I have had times when I thought it would be pleasant if I did not have to go on. [DECEMBER 1958]

Being a dog lover, do you condone scientific vivisection?

Certainly, when it is scientific and when proper consideration is given to caring for the animal and preventing any unnecessary suffering. [JANUARY 1960]

Don't you think if people learned to say "cancer" without shuddering or whispering, more victims would consult physicians when the first significant symptoms appear?

Yes, I think you are right, and I think the sooner we learn that cancer is curable if recognized in time, the greater the chances of curing and saving more people who suffer from this disease. [MAY 1947]

Recently, it seems that tremendous publicity is being given to any disease—especially cancer—that strikes a person who's in the public eye. Don't you think it would be in better taste to allow public figures a measure of decent privacy in such matters? How did your husband feel about having his illnesses publicized?

My husband knew there was no way he could hide the fact that he had polio. There is so much interest in whatever affects the President that it is impossible to keep news out of the papers, for what affects him affects the people. However, I sometimes think the details are too minutely described, and a little more restraint would be in better taste. But I believe the public does have a right to know about the health of a public servant. [AUGUST 1959]

Perhaps just as a footnote for history, would you be willing to say now whether, in your opinion, Mr. Roosevelt was in sufficiently good health to run for a fourth term?

All the doctors who examined my husband said he could run safely if he would observe certain rules for rest and relaxation. Of course, one never knows whether one can observe these rules at all times. However, if a man is deeply interested in the work he is doing, it is probably as injurious to his health to remove this interest as to have him continue, even if he cannot always follow doctor's orders. I would not feel I had sufficient knowledge to have an opinion on this particular question. [APRIL 1961]

I dread the change of life. How did you keep it from interfering with your busy life?

It is largely a question of really being busy and keeping oneself interested. I know there are abnormal cases, but for the ordinary woman it is quite easy to carry on life in a perfectly normal ordinary way. Discomforts are involved, but if you are busy and keep up your interests the discomforts will hardly be noticed. [JULY 1951]

I read that you went on a diet and lost over 20 pounds. I would like to know your diet as I am also 70 and have been told that dieting would be harmful at my age.

I suppose you should not diet without your doctor's consent, but my diet was very simple. I simply drank less and ate less! I never drink liquor or much wine, but I drank even fewer fluids generally and ate no starches and very moderately of other things. [MAY 1956]

It seems to me that you've increased your pace, not slackened it, as you've grown older. Is that true?

I have really never thought about whether I have increased or slackened my pace. One always goes a little slower as one grows older. I find I sleep on the train and am a little drowsy now and then, which did not happen when I was younger. But I also feel that with age I have fewer things the matter with me. I don't get colds so easily or headaches, which means that in a general way I am more dependable, because I rarely have to stop doing anything because of health.

On the whole I feel sure I am doing as much, if not more, than I did when I was younger. One reason, of course, is that I have fewer home duties. Since I live alone and really have only myself to think about in great part, I can do more of the things which other people ask me to do. [NOVEMBER 1954]

Why do you lead such an exhausting, busy life when you don't have to?

Because I like to work and to feel that I am being useful. When I am not well enough to do so, I will have to stop. In the meantime I enjoy a busy life. [APRIL 1957]

At what age do you hope to retire from public life?

I never plan ahead. [OCTOBER 1952]

ACKNOWLEDGMENTS

W RITING A BOOK is a lonely occupation, even with a subject as compelling as Eleanor Roosevelt. Fortunately, I have had the help and support of many staunch colleagues and good friends who have made this project a companionable one.

My first debt is to the literary estate of Eleanor Roosevelt and the estate's executor Nancy Roosevelt Ireland for permission to include excerpts from the "If You Ask Me" columns. I also want to thank the staff of the Eleanor Roosevelt Papers Project, particularly Christopher Brick, the project director, and Dr. Christy Regenhardt, for giving me permission to use the electronic transcripts of the column from the digital edition. I also thank them for their careful reading of the manuscript and for their friendship. Any errors that remain are mine.

As the supervisory editor of the digital edition, I worked with several very talented graduate and undergraduate students at the project's academic home, George Washington University. I especially want to acknowledge Elena Popchock, who helped organize the project and built the edition's website. Her efforts contributed significantly to the success of the final product. I would also like to thank five other graduate students: Felix Harcourt, M. Scott Heerman, Ruby Johnson, Seth LaShier, and Andreas Meyer. Their intelligence, diligence, and unfailing good cheer enriched this project and my life. Among the legion of undergraduates who worked on the digital edition, I thank Claire Crawford, Jay Fondin, Calla Gilson, Britt Lock-hart, Shelby Logan, Isabel Maier, and Donna Ra'anan-Lerner.

I also want to thank Allida Black, the founding director of the Eleanor Roosevelt Papers Project, for her faith in me, and Charlene Bickford, editor of the First Federal Congress Project, who taught me the rudiments of documentary editing and encouraged me to pursue a career in the field.

Claude Marx and Karen McNeilly read the manuscript and suggested several important changes. Thank you both.

I also want to acknowledge the hard work of my agents at Javelin, Keith Urbahn, Matt Latimer, and Dylan Colligan. Their determination to make this book a reality did much to stimulate my own enthusiasm, and I thank them for their encouragement and advocacy on my behalf.

The staff at Atria, particularly my editor Daniella Wexler, Peter Boland, Albert Tang, Dana Sloan, Katie Haigler, Audrey Sussman, Jim Walsh, and Sherry Wasserman have been unstinting in their efforts to make this a book to be proud of. Thank you. I also want to thank Paul Olsewski and Bianca Savant for their efforts to promote and market the book.

Many wise and devoted friends have sustained me as I worked on this project. For their constant support and encouragement, I thank Chris Alhambra, Rachel Bayley, Molly Bensinger-Lacy, the late Diane Lobb Boyce, Lynn Criste, Kristi Hiaasen, Mercedes Krcma, Susan Gates, Aaron and Debbie Goerlich, Susan Gonzalez, Anne West Kulick, Kristie Miller, John and Anne Mularoni, Bill and Mary Rawson, Richard and Anne Rodgers, Elise Schoux, Jamil and Lynn Sopher, and Michael Weeks. My parents Tony and Dede Casciato were enthusiastic supporters of my work; I am only sorry they are not here to see the results. My siblings, Tom and Nancy Casciato; their spouses, Kathleen Hughes and Kenn Walton; and Tom's sons, Peter and William, have also been invaluable sources of support and advice. I deeply regret that my brother Peter died before I began work on this manuscript. However, his wife, Regina, and their children, Zach, Sam, and Victoria, keep his memory bright and are in themselves sources of never-ending joy.

Lastly, I thank my son, Tony, whose gridiron career has provided a welcome break from the rigors of research and writing. As for my husband, Roland, without his common sense, optimism, and computer skills, this project and much else in my life would never have happened.

NOTES

INTRODUCTION

1. This book is based on the full text of the column but does not include every question and answer. All the columns are available on the Eleanor Roosevelt Papers Project website at https://erpapers.columbian .gwu.edu/if-you-ask-me-0.

2. Joseph P. Lash, *Eleanor Roosevelt: A Friend's Memoir* (Garden City, NY: Doubleday & Company, Inc., 1964), 39.

3. Cathy D. Knepper, *Dear Mrs. Roosevelt: Letters to Eleanor Roosevelt Through Depression and War* (New York: Carroll & Graf, 2004), xv, xviii.

4. Kathleen Endes, *"Ladies Home Journal"* and *"McCall's,"* in Maurine H. Beasley et al., eds., *The Eleanor Roosevelt Encyclopedia* (Westport, CT: Greenwood Press, 2001), 298–301, 333–335; Peter Bart, "Advertising: 2 Magazine Dowagers Battle," *New York Times*, July 30, 1961, F12.

5. Eleanor Roosevelt, "If You Ask Me," *Ladies Home Journal*, vol. 59, 31, February 1942 and August 1943, in The Eleanor Roosevelt Papers Digital Edition.

6. Eleanor Roosevelt, *If You Ask Me* (D. Appleton-Century Co., Inc., 1946); Eleanor Roosevelt, *It Seems to Me* (New York: W. W. Norton, 1954).

7. Allida M. Black et al., eds., *The Eleanor Roosevelt Papers, Vol. 2: The Human Rights Years, 1949–1952* (Charlottesville, VA: The University of Virginia Press, 2012), xxxvii.

8. Eleanor Roosevelt, *Eleanor Roosevelt's Book of Common Sense Etiquette* (New York: MacMillan Co., 1962), x.

9. Eleanor Roosevelt, "My Day," June 22, 1944, in The Eleanor Roosevelt Papers Digital Edition.

10. Eleanor Roosevelt, "Tolerance Is an Ugly Word," in Allida M. Black et al., eds., *The Eleanor Roosevelt Papers, Vol. 1: The Human Rights Years, 1945–1948* (Detroit: Thomson Gale, 2007), 56.

11. Roosevelt, "My Day," October 25, 1945, in The Eleanor Roosevelt Papers Digital Edition.

Chapter 1: WOMEN AND GENDER

1. Paul Boyer, *Promises to Keep: The United States Since World War II* (Lexington, MA: D.C. Heath and Co., 1995), 24–25, 71, 94–95.

2. Blanche Wiesen Cook, *Eleanor Roosevelt, Vol. 2: 1933–1938* (New York: Viking, 1999), 74; Kelly A. Woestman, "President's Commission on the Status of Women," in Maurine H. Beasley et al., eds., *The Eleanor Roosevelt Encyclopedia* (Westport, CT: Greenwood Press, 2001), 407–411.

3. Eleanor Roosevelt, "My Day," August 7, 1941, and August 25, 1945, in The Eleanor Roosevelt Papers Digital Edition.

4. Ruth Rosen, *The World Split Open: How the Modern Women's Movement Changed America* (New York: Viking, 2000), 19–20; Roosevelt, "My Day," June 12, 1961, in The Eleanor Roosevelt Digital Edition.

5. Scharf, "Equal Rights Amendment," in Beasley et al., eds., *The Eleanor Roosevelt Encyclopedia*, 161–165; Roosevelt, "My Day," May, 25, 1951, in The Eleanor Roosevelt Papers Digital Edition.

Chapter 2: RACE AND ETHNICITY

1. Joanna Schneider Zangrando and Robert L. Zangrando, "ER and Black Civil Rights," in Joan Hoff-Wilson and Marjorie Lightman, eds., *Without Precedent: The Life and Career of Eleanor Roosevelt* (Bloomington, IN: University of Indiana Press, 1984), 88; Eleanor Roosevelt, "If You Ask Me," *Ladies Home Journal*, August 1941; "If You Ask Me," *McCall's*, August 1956; "If You Ask Me," *Ladies Home Journal*, June 1942; "If You Ask Me," *Ladies Home Journal*, April 1944 and November 1944; "If You Ask Me," *Ladies Home Journal*, November 1948, in The Eleanor Roosevelt Papers Digital Edition.

2. Eleanor Roosevelt, "My Day," December 16, 1941, in The Eleanor Roosevelt Papers Digital Edition.

3. Eleanor Roosevelt, "The Minorities Question," in Allida M. Black et al., eds., *The Eleanor Roosevelt Papers, Vol. 1: The Human Rights Years, 1945–1948* (Farmington Hills, MI: Thomson-Gale, 2007), 392–395.

4. Eleanor Roosevelt, *Tomorrow Is Now* (New York: Harper & Row, 1963), 19.

5. Ibid., 51.

6. Jerome A. Chanes, *Antisemitism: A Reference Handbook* (Santa Barbara: ABC-CLIO, Inc., 2004,) 74–75; Albert S. Lindemann and Richard S. Levy, *Antisemitism: A History* (New York: Oxford University Press, 2010), 159–161.

7. Eleanor Roosevelt, "Keepers of Democracy," *Virginia Quarterly Review*, January 1939, 3.

Chapter 3: **POLITICS AND ECONOMICS**

1. Eleanor Roosevelt, *You Learn by Living: Eleven Keys for a More Fulfilling Life* (Louisville, KY: Westminster John Knox Press, 1960), 171.

2. Blanche Wiesen Cook, *Eleanor Roosevelt, Vol. 1: 1884–1933* (New York: Viking, 1992), 339–340.

3. Roosevelt, *You Learn by Living*, 174–175.

4. Paul Boyer, *Promises to Keep: The United States Since World War II* (Lexington, MA: D.C. Heath and Co., 1995), 72–73, 75–76, 92–93, 124–125; Joshua B. Freeman, "Labor," in Eric Foner and John A. Garraty, eds., *The Reader's Companion to American History* (Boston, MA: Houghton Mifflin, 1991), 633.

5. Brigid O'Farrell, *She Was One of Us: Eleanor Roosevelt and the American Worker* (Ithaca, NY: Cornell University Press, 2010), 1–3; Robert H. Zieger and Anders G. Lewis, "Labor," in Maurine H. Beasley et al., eds., *The Eleanor Roosevelt Encyclopedia* (Westport, CT: Greenwood Press, 2001), 294–298; Eleanor Roosevelt, "My Day," March 19, 1936, in The Eleanor Roosevelt Papers Digital Edition.

6. Alan Brinkley, *The Unfinished Nation: A Concise History of the United States* (New York: Alfred A. Knopf, 1997), 712–714; "Huey Pierce Long,

American Politician," Encyclopedia Britannica Online, s.v., https://www.britannica.com/biography/Huey-Long-American-politician (accessed October 8, 2017).

7. Ellen W. Schrecker, "Joseph R. McCarthy," in Foner and Garraty, eds., *The Reader's Companion to American History*, 709–710; Joseph P. Lash, *Eleanor: The Years Alone* (New York: W. W. Norton & Co., Inc., 1972), 233–234; Richard M. Fried, "McCarthyism," in Beasley et al., eds., *The Eleanor Roosevelt Encyclopedia*, 335–337.

8. "Electing the President," *New York Times*, February 1, 1950, 28; "The 'College' Survives," *New York Times*, July 18, 1950, 28; David Halberstam, "District of Columbia Vote Gains As 36th State Backs Amendment," *New York Times*, March 23, 1961, 26; "Capital's Vote Is Law," *New York Times*, April 4, 1961, 24.

9. "Nelson Aldrich Rockefeller," Encyclopedia Britannica Online, s.v., https://www.britannica.com/biography/Nelson-Aldrich-Rockefeller (accessed October 8, 2017); "Barry Goldwater, United States Senator," Encyclopedia Britannica Online, s.v., https://www.britannica.com/biography/Barry-Goldwater (accessed October 8, 2017).

10. James Patterson, "Robert S. McNamara," American National Biography Online, s.v., http://www.anb.org.proxygw.wrlc.org/view/10.1093/anb/9780198606697.001.0001/anb-9780198606697-e-0700827?rskey=k61gYm&result=1 (accessed February 1, 2018).

11. Kristie Miller, "William Averell Harriman," in Beasley et al., eds., *The Eleanor Roosevelt Encyclopedia*, 228–230; Lash, *Eleanor*, 254–256; Eleanor Roosevelt, "If You Ask Me," *McCall's*, July 1960, in The Eleanor Roosevelt Papers Digital Edition.

12. William J. Eaton, "Walter Philip Reuther," in Beasley et al., eds., *The Eleanor Roosevelt Encyclopedia*, 440–442.

13. "Arthur M. Schlesinger, Jr.," Encyclopedia Britannica Online, s.v., https://www.britannica.com/biography/Arthur-M-Schlesinger-Jr (accessed February 1, 2018).

14. Robert Dallek, *Franklin D. Roosevelt: A Political Life* (New York: Viking, 2017), 571; Doris Kearns Goodwin, *No Ordinary Time: Franklin and Eleanor Roosevelt: The Home Front in World War II* (New York:

Simon & Schuster, 1994), 525–526; James H. Madison, "Wendell Lewis Willkie," *American National Biography Online*, s.v., http://www.anb.org.proxygw.wrlc.org/articles/06/06-00718.html?a=1&n=Wendell%20Willkie&d=10&ss=0&q=1 (accessed November 26, 2017); Conrad Black, *Franklin Delano Roosevelt: Champion of Freedom* (New York: PublicAffairs, 2003), 455–460, 951–952.

15. Eleanor Roosevelt, "Why I Do Not Choose to Run," *Look*, July 9, 1946, in Allida M. Black et al., eds., *The Eleanor Roosevelt Papers, Vol. 1: The Human Rights Years, 1945–1948* (Farmington Hills, MI: Thomson-Gale, 2007), 359–361; Lash, *Eleanor*, 139.

Chapter 4: CIVIL LIBERTIES

1. In the 1930s, while first lady, Eleanor Roosevelt had worked with reform student groups thinking they would be potential allies and counterweights to more conservative political influences on F.D.R. and the Congress. When, in 1940, the groups were found to have communist links, she withdrew her support. Melissa Walker, "American Student Union," Eileen Eagan, "American Youth Congress," and Richard Gid Powers, "Federal Bureau of Investigation," in Maurine H. Beasley et al., eds., *The Eleanor Roosevelt Encyclopedia* (Westport, CT: Greenwood Press, 2001), 14–16, 16–19, 172–176.

2. Paul Boyer, *Promises to Keep: The United States Since World War II* (Lexington, MA: D.C. Heath and Co., 1995), 88–89.

3. Eleanor Roosevelt, "If You Ask Me," *McCall's*, July 1953, in The Eleanor Roosevelt Papers Digital Edition.

4. Eleanor Roosevelt, "If You Ask Me," *Ladies Home Journal*, February 1948, in The Eleanor Roosevelt Papers Digital Edition.

5. Eleanor Roosevelt, "Freedom of Speech Broadcast," October 14, 1941, quoted in Tamara K. Hareven, *Eleanor Roosevelt: An American Conscience* (Chicago: Quadrangle Books, 1968), 165.

6. Eleanor Roosevelt, "If You Ask Me," *Ladies Home Journal*, February 1949, in The Eleanor Roosevelt Papers Digital Edition.

Chapter 5: **LOVE, MARRIAGE, AND FAMILY**

1. Sheri Stritof, "Estimated Median Age of First Marriage by Gender, 1890–2015," The Spruce, https://www.thespruce.com/estimated-median-age-marriage-2303878 (accessed October 13, 2017); "Table MS-2: "Estimated Median Age at First Marriage, 1890 to the Present," U.S. Census Bureau, 2011, https://www.census.gov/content/dam/Census/library/visualizations/time-series/demo/families-and-households/ms-2.pdf (accessed September 1, 2017); Paul Boyer, *Promises to Keep: The United States Since World War II* (Lexington, MA: D.C. Heath and Co., 1995), 92–93; Robert H. Bremmer and Gary W. Reichard, eds., *Reshaping America: Society and Institutions 1945–1960* (Columbus: Ohio State University Press, 1982), 10, 13.

2. Bremmer and Reichard, *Reshaping America*, 8–10; Alexandra Nikolchev, "A Brief History of the Birth Control Pill," *Need to Know on PBS*, May 7, 2010, http://www.pbs.org/wnet/need-to-know/health/a-brief-history-of-the-birth-control-pill/480/ (accessed October 10, 2017); James C. Mohr, "Abortion," in Eric Foner and John A. Garraty, eds., *The Reader's Companion to American History* (Boston, MA: Houghton Mifflin, 1991), 3–5.

3. After 1946, the divorce rate dropped and then leveled off in the 1950s and early '60s. It rose again after Eleanor's death. Shawn Garrison, "Examining Marriage & Divorce Rates Throughout U.S. History," Dads Divorce, https://dadsdivorce.com/articles/examining-marriage-divorce-rates-throughout-u-s-history/ (accessed February 1, 2018); Robert L. Griswald, "Divorce," in Foner and Garraty, eds., *The Reader's Companion to American History*, 288; Boyer, *Promises to Keep*, 147–151.

4. Eleanor Roosevelt, "If You Ask Me," *Ladies Home Journal*, September 1944 and January 1945, in The Eleanor Roosevelt Papers Digital Edition.

5. Blanche Wiesen Cook, *Eleanor Roosevelt, Vol. 1: 1884–1933* (New York: Viking, 1992), 227–232; Doris Kearns Goodwin, *No Ordinary Time: Franklin and Eleanor Roosevelt: The Home Front in World War II* (New York: Simon & Schuster, 1994), 517–518.

Chapter 6: **RELIGION AND FAITH**

1. Paul Boyer, *Promises to Keep: The United States Since World War II* (Lexington, MA: D.C. Heath and Co., 1995), 134–135; Robert H. Bremmer and Gary W. Reichard, eds., *Reshaping America: Society and Institutions 1945–1960* (Columbus: Ohio State University Press, 1982), 173–174.
2. Eleanor Roosevelt, "What Religion Means to Me," *Forum*, December 1932, 324.

Chapter 7: **ETIQUETTE**

1. Nancy A. Walker, *Shaping Our Mothers' World: American Women's Magazines* (Jackson, MS: University Press of Mississippi, 2000), 139–141.
2. Eleanor Roosevelt, "If You Ask Me," *Ladies Home Journal*, February 1942 and October 1946; Eleanor Roosevelt, "If You Ask Me," *McCall's*, February 1955 and March 1959, in The Eleanor Roosevelt Papers Digital Edition.
3. Eleanor Roosevelt had made the same point in a 1939 article for the *Ladies Home Journal*. See Eleanor Roosevelt, "Good Manners," *Ladies Home Journal*, vol. 56, June 1939, 21, 116–117; Eleanor Roosevelt, *Eleanor Roosevelt's Book of Common Sense Etiquette* (New York: The MacMillan Co., 1962), ix–x.
4. Eleanor Roosevelt, *Tomorrow Is Now* (New York: Harper & Row, 1963), 88.

Chapter 8: **YOUTH, POPULAR CULTURE, AND EDUCATION**

1. Eleanor Roosevelt and Helen Ferris, *Your Teens and Mine* (Garden City, NY: Doubleday & Company, Inc., 1961), 40–45, 77; Paul Boyer, *Promises to Keep: The United States Since World War II* (Lexington, MA: D.C. Heath and Co., 1995), 150.
2. Eleanor Roosevelt, "If You Ask Me," *Ladies Home Journal*, December 1942 and July 1946, in The Eleanor Roosevelt Papers Digital Edition; Eleanor Roosevelt's commercial for Good Luck margarine can be found

at Youtube: "Eleanor Roosevelt Margarine Commercial," 1959, Youtube, 0:27, https://www.youtube.com/watch?v=6HY8vxYX78s (accessed October 20, 2017); Thomas Louis Stix, "Mrs. Roosevelt Does a TV Commercial," *Harper's*, November 1963, https://harpers.org/archive/1963/11/mrs-roosevelt-does-a-tv-commercial/ (accessed October 1, 2017).

3. Eleanor Roosevelt, "If You Ask Me," *Ladies Home Journal*, May 1942 and May 1943, in The Eleanor Roosevelt Papers Digital Edition.

4. Roosevelt, "If You Ask Me," *Ladies Home Journal*, December 1941 and July 1944, in The Eleanor Roosevelt Papers Digital Edition.

5. Alan Brinkley, *The Unfinished Nation: A Concise History of the United States* (New York: Alfred A. Knopf, 1997), 812–813; Nancy Woloch, "Education," in Eric Foner and John A. Garraty, eds., *The Reader's Companion to American History* (Boston, MA: Houghton Mifflin, 1991), 319; Roosevelt, "If You Ask Me," *McCalls*, April 1961, and *Ladies Home Journal*, November 1942, in The Eleanor Roosevelt Papers Digital Edition.

6. Eleanor Roosevelt, "My Day," December 22, 1945, in The Eleanor Roosevelt Papers Digital Edition.

7. Eleanor Roosevelt, *Tomorrow Is Now* (New York: Harper & Row, 1963), 73.

8. Charles B. Gould and Beatrice Blackmar Gould, *American Story: Memories and Reflections of Bruce Gould and Beatrice Blackmar Gould* (New York: Harper & Row, 1968), 214.

9. Frank Freidel, *Franklin D. Roosevelt: A Rendezvous with Destiny* (Boston, MA: Back Bay Books, 1990), 558.

10. See, for example, Roosevelt, "My Day," September 3, 1946; January 14, 1953; December 5, 1956; and January 29, 1960, in The Eleanor Roosevelt Papers Digital Edition.

Chapter 9: **WAR AND PEACE**

1. Eleanor Roosevelt, "Liberals in This Year of Decision," *Christian Register*, June 1948, Eleanor Roosevelt Papers Project, https://erpapers.columbian.gwu.edu/liberals-year-decision (accessed June 15, 2018).

2. Eleanor Roosevelt, *Tomorrow Is Now* (New York: Harper & Row, 1963), 75.

3. Eleanor Roosevelt, *You Learn By Living: Eleven Keys to a More Fulfilling Life* (Louisville, KY: Westminster John Knox Press, 1960), 117.

4. Paul Boyer, *Promises to Keep: The United States Since World War II* (Lexington, MA: D.C. Heath and Co., 1995), 24; Steven Mintz, "Family," in Eric Foner and John A. Garraty, eds., *The Reader's Companion to American History* (Boston, MA: Houghton Mifflin, 1991), 378–382; Doris Kearns Goodwin, *No Ordinary Time: Franklin and Eleanor Roosevelt: The Home Front in World War II* (New York: Simon & Schuster, 1994), 365, 413–414.

5. In 1943, the WAAC was merged into the Army, and the name was changed to the Women's Army Corps (WAC). That same year, detractors started a whispering campaign to portray women who had joined as camp followers, i.e., prostitutes or lesbians. "The WAAC Whisper Campaign," Homefront Heroines, http://www.homefrontheroines.com/exhibits/changing-attitudes/the-rumor-mill/the-waac-whisper-campaign/ (accessed October 3, 2017).

6. Richard Breitman and Allan Lichtman, *FDR and the Jews* (Boston, MA: Harvard University Press, 2013), 4; Hasia R. Diner, "Jews," in Maurine H. Beasley et al., eds., *The Eleanor Roosevelt Encyclopedia* (Westport, CT: Greenwood Press, 2001), 281–284; "Roosevelt Sets Up War Refugee Board," *New York Times*, January 23, 1944, 11; "War Refugee Board," United States Holocaust Memorial Museum, www.ushmm.org/outreach/en/article.php?ModuleId=10007749 (accessed February 1, 2018).

7. Anna Kasten Nelson and Sara E. Wilson, "Cold War," in Beasley et al., eds., *The Eleanor Roosevelt Encyclopedia*, 100–103; Eleanor Roosevelt, "The Russians Are Tough," *Look*, February 18, 1947, printed in Allida M. Black et al., eds., *The Eleanor Roosevelt Papers, Vol. 1: The Human Rights Years, 1945–1948* (Farmington Hills, MI: Thomson-Gale, 2007), 511–513.

8. Frank Gibney, "Nikita Sergeyevich Khrushchev," Encyclopedia Britannica Online, s.v., https://www.britannica.com/biography/Nikita-Sergeyevich-Khrushchev (accessed February 11, 2018); "Nikita Khrushchev (1894–1971)," PBS, http://www.pbs.org/redfiles/bios/all_bio_nikita_khrushchev.htm (accessed February 11, 2018); Joseph P. Lash, *Eleanor: The Years Alone* (New York: W. W. Norton & Co., Inc., 1972), 270–274.

9. Gregory Freidin, "Boris Leonidovich Pasternak," Encyclopedia Britannica Online, s.v., https://www.britannica.com/biography/Boris-Pasternak (accessed February 11, 2018); Lash, *Eleanor*, 272.

10. Robert D. McFadden, "Vincent Impellitteri Is Dead; Mayor of New York in 1950s," *New York Times*, January 30, 1987, B8.

11. William Manchester and Paul Reid, *The Last Lion: Winston Spencer Churchill: Defender of the Realm, 1940–1965* (New York: Little, Brown & Co., 2012), 960–961; Eleanor Roosevelt, "My Day," March 7 and 27, 1946, in The Eleanor Roosevelt Papers Digital Edition; Drew Pearson, "Washington Merry-Go-Round," *Washington Post*, March 23, 1946, 7.

12. Eleanor Roosevelt, "If You Ask Me," *McCall's*, March 1956, in The Eleanor Roosevelt Papers Digital Edition; Eleanor Roosevelt, *On My Own* (New York: Harper & Brothers, 1958), 71.

13. Eleanor Roosevelt, "Address to the Democratic National Convention," July 22, 1952, quoted in Allida M. Black, et al., eds., *The Eleanor Roosevelt Papers, Vol. 2: The Human Rights Years, 1949–1952*, (Charlottesville: University of Virginia Press, 2012), 907–913.

14. Felice D. Gaer, "American Association for the United Nations," in Beasley et al., eds., *The Eleanor Roosevelt Encyclopedia*, 5–8; Jean Harvey Baker, "United Nations," in Beasley et al., eds., *The Eleanor Roosevelt Encyclopedia*, 534–539.

Chapter 10: **HEALTH AND AGING**

1. Medicine and Madison Avenue On-Line Project, John W. Harman Center for Advertising & Marketing History, David M. Rubenstein Rare Book & Manuscript Library, Duke University, Durham, North Carolina, https://library.duke.edu/digitalcollections/mma/timeline/ (accessed January 25, 2018); Albert M. Cole, "What the Aged Need in Their Homes," *New York Times*, August 4, 1957, SM6.

2. Eleanor Roosevelt, *Eleanor Roosevelt's Book of Common Sense Etiquette* (New York: MacMillan Co., 1962), 66.

3. Blanche Wiesen Cook, *Eleanor Roosevelt, Vol. 1: 1884–1933* (New York: Viking, 1992), 249.

4. Joseph P. Lash, *"Life Was Meant to Be Lived": A Centenary Portrait of Eleanor Roosevelt* (New York: W. W. Norton & Co., 1984), 184; Eleanor Roosevelt, "My Day," November 7, 1958, in The Eleanor Roosevelt Papers Digital Edition.

5. Eleanor Roosevelt to David Gray, April 11, 1956, David Gray Papers, Eleanor Roosevelt Papers General Correspondence, 1955–1962, and undated, Box 6, Franklin D. Roosevelt Presidential Library, Hyde Park, New York.

6. Jay Allison and Dan Gediman, eds., *This I Believe: The Personal Philosophies of Remarkable Men and Women* (New York: Henry Holt, 2006), 203.

BIBLIOGRAPHY

BOOKS

Albion, Michele Wehrwein, ed. *The Quotable Eleanor Roosevelt.* Gainesville: University Press of Florida, 2013.

Beasley, Maurine C., Holly C. Shulman, and Henry R. Beasley, eds. *The Eleanor Roosevelt Encyclopedia.* Westport, CT: Greenwood Press, 2001.

Black, Allida M. *Courage in a Dangerous World: The Political Writings of Eleanor Roosevelt.* New York: Columbia University Press, 1999.

———, John F. Sears, Mary Jo Binker, Craig Daigle, Michael Weeks, and Christopher Alhambra, eds. *The Eleanor Roosevelt Papers, Vol. 1: The Human Rights Years, 1945–1948.* Farmington Hills, MI: Thomson-Gale, 2007.

———, Mary Jo Binker, Christopher Brick, Robert P. Frankel Jr., and Christy Regenhardt, eds. *The Eleanor Roosevelt Papers, Vol. 2: The Human Rights Years, 1949–1952.* Charlottesville: University of Virginia Press, 2012.

Black, Conrad. *Franklin Delano Roosevelt: Champion of Freedom.* New York: PublicAffairs, 2003.

Boyer, Paul. *Promises to Keep: The United States Since World War II.* Lexington, MA: D.C. Heath and Co., 1995.

Breitman, Richard, and Allan Lichtman. *FDR and the Jews.* Boston: Harvard University Press, 2013.

Bremmer, Robert H., and Gary W. Reichard, eds. *Reshaping America: Society and Institutions 1945–1960.* Columbus: Ohio State University Press, 1982.

Brinkley, Alan. *The Unfinished Nation: A Concise History of the United States.* New York: Alfred A. Knopf, 1997.

Chanes, Jerome A. *Antisemitism: A Reference Handbook.* Santa Barbara, CA: ABC-CLIO, Inc., 2004.

Cook, Blanche Wiesen. *Eleanor Roosevelt, Vol. 1: 1884–1933.* New York: Viking, 1992.

———. *Eleanor Roosevelt, Vol. 2: 1933–1938.* New York: Viking, 1999.

Dallek, Robert, *Franklin D. Roosevelt: A Political Life.* New York: Viking, 2017.

Foner, Eric, and John A. Garraty, eds. *The Reader's Companion to American History.* Boston: Houghton Mifflin, 1991.

Freidel, Frank. *Franklin D. Roosevelt: A Rendezvous with Destiny.* Boston: Back Bay Books, 1990.

Goodwin, Doris Kearns. *No Ordinary Time: Franklin and Eleanor Roosevelt: The Home Front in World War II.* New York: Simon & Schuster, 1995.

Gould, Charles B., and Beatrice Blackmar Gould. *American Story: Memories and Reflections of Bruce Gould and Beatrice Blackmar Gould.* New York: Harper & Row, 1968.

Hareven, Tamara K. *Eleanor Roosevelt: An American Conscience.* Chicago: Quadrangle Books, 1968.

Hoff-Wilson, Joan, and Marjorie Lightman, eds. *Without Precedent: The Life and Career of Eleanor Roosevelt.* Bloomington: University of Indiana Press, 1984.

Knepper, Cathy D. *Dear Mrs. Roosevelt: Letters to Eleanor Roosevelt Through Depression and War.* New York: Carroll & Graf, 2004.

Lash, Joseph P. *Eleanor: The Years Alone.* New York: W. W. Norton & Co., Inc., 1972.

———. *Eleanor Roosevelt: A Friend's Memoir.* Garden City, NY: Doubleday & Company, Inc., 1964).

———. *"Life Was Meant to Be Lived": A Centenary Portrait of Eleanor Roosevelt,* New York: W. W. Norton & Co., 1984.

Lindemann, Albert S., and Richard S. Levy. *Antisemitism: A History.* New York: Oxford University Press, 2010.

Manchester, William, and Paul Reid, *The Last Lion: Winston Spencer*

Churchill: Defender of the Realm, 1940–1965. New York: Little, Brown & Co., 2012.

O'Farrell, Brigid. *She Was One of Us: Eleanor Roosevelt and the American Worker.* Ithaca, NY: Cornell University Press, 2017.

Roosevelt, Eleanor. *Eleanor Roosevelt's Book of Common Sense Etiquette.* New York: The MacMillan Co., 1962.

———. *If You Ask Me.* New York: D. Appleton-Century Co., Inc., 1946.

———. *It Seems to Me.* New York: W. W. Norton, 1954.

———. *Tomorrow Is Now.* New York: Harper & Row, 1963.

———. *On My Own.* New York: Harper & Brothers, 1958.

———. *You Learn By Living: Eleven Keys for a More Fulfilling Life.* Louisville, KY: Westminster John Knox Press, 1960.

——— and Helen Ferris. *Your Teens and Mine.* Garden City, NY: Doubleday & Company, Inc., 1961.

Rosen, Ruth. *The World Split Open: How the Modern Women's Movement Changed America.* New York: Viking, 2000.

Walker, Nancy A. *Shaping Our Mothers' World: American Women's Magazines.* Jackson, MS: University Press of Mississippi, 2000.

ARTICLES

Bart, Peter. "Advertising: 2 Magazine Dowagers Battle." *New York Times,* July 30, 1961, F12.

Cole, Albert M. "What the Aged Need in Their Homes." *New York Times,* August 4, 1957, SM6.

Halberstam, David. "District of Columbia Vote Gains As 36th State Backs Amendment." *New York Times,* March 23, 1961, 26.

McFadden, Robert D. "Vincent Impellitteri Is Dead; Mayor of New York in 1950s." *New York Times,* January 30, 1987, B8.

New York Times. "Capital's Vote Is Law." April 4, 1961, 24.

———. "The 'College' Survives." July 18, 1950, 28.

———. "Electing the President." February 1, 1950, 28.

———. "Roosevelt Sets Up War Refugee Board." January 23, 1944, 11.

Pearson, Drew. "Washington Merry-Go-Round." *Washington Post*, March 23, 1946, 7.

Roosevelt, Eleanor. "Good Manners." *Ladies Home Journal*, vol. 56, June 1939, 116–117.

———. "Keepers of Democracy." *Virginia Quarterly Review*, vol. 15, January 1939, 1–5.

———. "Liberals in This Year of Decision," *Christian Register*, June 1948.

———. "What Religion Means to Me." *Forum*, December 1932.

ONLINE SOURCES

American National Biography Online. http://www.anb.org.

The Eleanor Roosevelt Papers Project. "If You Ask Me." The Eleanor Roosevelt Papers Digital Edition. https://erpapers.columbian.gwu.edu/if -you-ask-me-0.

———. "My Day." The Eleanor Roosevelt Papers Digital Edition. https:// erpapers.columbian.gwu.edu/my-day.

Encyclopedia Britannica Online. https://www.britannica.com.

Garrison, Shawn. "Examining Marriage & Divorce Rates Throughout U.S. History." Dads Divorce. Accessed February 1, 2018. https:// dadsdivorce.com/articles/examining-marriage-divorce-rates-throughout -u-s-history/.

Homefront Heroines. "The WAAC Whisper Campaign." http://www .homefrontheroines.com/exhibits/changing-attitudes/the-rumor-mill /the-waac-whisper-campaign/.

Medicine and Madison Avenue On-Line Project. John W. Harman Center for Advertising & Marketing History, David M. Rubenstein Rare Book & Manuscript Library, Duke University. Durham, North Carolina.

Nikolchev, Alexandra. "A Brief History of the Birth Control Pill." *Need to Know on PBS*, May 7, 2010. http://www.pbs.org/wnet/need-to-know /health/a-brief-history-of-the-birth-control-pill/480/.

Good Luck Margarine. "Eleanor Roosevelt Margarine Commercial." Television advertisement. Ogilvy & Mather, 1959. https://www.youtube .com/watch?v=6HY8vxYX78s.

PBS. "Nikita Khrushchev (1894–1971)." http://www.pbs.org/redfiles/bios/all_bio_nikita_khrushchev.htm (accessed February 11, 2018).

Stix, Thomas Louis. "Mrs. Roosevelt Does a TV Commercial." *Harper's*, November 1963. https://harpers.org/archive/1963/11/mrs-roosevelt-does-a-tv-commercial/.

Stritof, Sheri. "Estimated Median Age of First Marriage By Gender 1890–2015." The Spruce. https://www.thespruce.com/estimated-median-age-marriage-2303878.

United States Holocaust Memorial Museum. "War Refugee Board." https://www.ushmm.org/outreach/en/article.php?ModuleId=10007749.

U.S. Census Bureau. "Table MS-2: "Estimated Median Age at First Marriage, 1890 to the Present." *2011.* https://www.census.gov/content/dam/Census/library/visualizations/time-series/demo/families-and-households/ms-2.pdf.

ADDITIONAL READING

In addition to the books in the bibliography about Eleanor Roosevelt, the following books and websites are also useful sources of information about her life and work.

BOOKS

Asbell, Bernard. *Mother and Daughter: The Letters of Eleanor and Anna Roosevelt.* New York: Fromm International Publishing Corp., 1988.

Beasley, Maurine H. *Eleanor Roosevelt and the Media: A Public Quest for Self-Fulfillment.* Urbana: University of Illinois Press, 1987.

Cook, Blanche Wiesen. *Eleanor Roosevelt: The War Years and After, 1939–1962, Vol. 3.* New York: Viking, 2016.

Glendon, Mary Ann. *A World Made New: Eleanor Roosevelt and the Universal Declaration of Human Rights.* New York: Random House, 2002.

Lash, Joseph P. *Eleanor and Franklin: The Story of Their Relationship Based on Eleanor Roosevelt's Private Papers.* New York: W. W. Norton & Co., Inc., 1971.

Quinn, Susan. *Eleanor and Hick: The Love Affair that Shaped a First Lady.* New York: Penguin Press, 2016.

Roosevelt, Eleanor. *The Autobiography of Eleanor Roosevelt.* New York: Harper Perennial, 2014.

———. *It's Up to the Women.* New York: Hachette, 2017.

———. *The Moral Basis of Democracy.* New York: Harper Perennial, 2014.

———. *Tomorrow Is Now.* New York, Penguin Books, 2012.

Rowley, Hazel. *Franklin and Eleanor: An Extraordinary Marriage.* New York: Farrar, Straus and Giroux, 2010.

Scott, Patricia Bell. *The Firebrand and the First Lady: Portrait of a Friendship: Pauli Murray, Eleanor Roosevelt, and the Struggle for Social Justice.* New York: Alfred A. Knopf, 2016.

Streitmatter, Rodger. *Empty Without You: The Intimate Letters of Eleanor Roosevelt and Lorena Hickok.* New York: Free Press, 1998.

WEBSITES

The Eleanor Roosevelt Papers Project. https://erpapers.columbian.gwu.edu/.
The Franklin D. Roosevelt Presidential Library. https://fdrlibrary.org/.

QUOTATION CREDITS

The quote from "Liberals in This Year of Decision" by Eleanor Roosevelt on page 174 is used with permission of the Unitarian Universalist Association.

The quotes from "The Minorities Question" on page 14 and "Tolerance Is an Ugly Word" on page xii from Allida Black. *THE ELEANOR ROOSEVELT PAPERS:HMN RGHTS & UN YRS V1 1945–48*, 1E. © 2007 Gale, a part of Cengage, Inc. Reproduced by permission. www.cengage.com/permissions

Quotes from *Tomorrow Is Now* on pages 14, 15, 118, 133, and 174 are considered fair use by Penguin Random House.

The quote from Blanche Wiesen Cook's *Eleanor Roosevelt, Volume 2: 1933–1938* on page 2 is considered fair use by Penguin Random House.